The Cl
Compa

Martin Mason
Malcolm Sanders

ROBERT HALE · LONDON

CONTENTS

I

INTRODUCTION

This book is intended as a guide for those people, whether tourists, commuters, or Londoners, who wish to spend time exploring the older nooks and crannies of the City of London, and discovering the wealth of architectural and historical interest that they contain.

For many visitors the 'square mile' is simply a modern financial and business centre, its pavements teeming with office workers, its streets clogged with traffic, and with St Paul's Cathedral and the City churches being the only obvious relics of the past. At a superficial glance this would appear to be true. On every hand one sees the trappings of a modern city, but London, like most cities, is an organic growth, the alteration and change of both its function and appearance being part of a continuing process, and surviving behind this late 20th. century facade are the remains of older cities.

The history of London is really the tale of three cities (and three distructions) the first being the medieval city that developed from the ruins of the Roman Londinium. For much of the period from the departure of the Roman legions to the Norman conquest of 1066, London existed as a border town, important as a commercial centre but of fluctuating political significance. It was only with the coming of the Normans that its status as the capital of England was permanently established. The medieval City, by and large, kept within the bounds set by the Roman walls, the major exception to this being the growth of the outpost of Southwark at the southern end of London Bridge. This was a centre for the vicious amusements of the time and a refuge for prostitutes, criminals, actors, and other undesirable elements. This City was an unplanned growth and to modern eyes would have seemed grossly over-crowded and appallingly insanitary. However, it was the city of Dick Whittington, Chaucer, Caxton, and Shakespeare, and with all its faults was recognised as being one of the major cities of Europe. This dynamic, teeming, rat infested hive of industry was destroyed almost totally in the Great Fire of 1666, and from its ashes a new city was to arise.

This new creation was not to be the rational planned city conceived by Sir Christopher Wren in the aftermath of the Fire. The new buildings that arose were of stone and brick and of a better standard of design and construction than their timber predecessors, but the old street pattern and ownership boundaries were largely retained. Although his grand plans for a baroque city failed to materialise, this new London was nevertheless very much Wren's creation. Its most notable feature was the soaring forest of spires rising from the fifty two churches for which he was responsible, the whole crowned by the majestic dome of St Paul's Cathedral. During the eighteenth century the City burst its bounds, the walls were breached and demolished, unable any more to withstand the overwhelming pressure from within. This resulted in the rapid expansion of the area known as the West End and other what are now inner suburbs, a development that was to lead inevitably and inexorably to the creation of the third city.

With the steady departure of the residential population to the new suburbs the way was clear for the development of the commercial and financial centre that we know today. This was a Victorian creation, a city that in the range of its architecture, from the refined and scholarly to the eccentric and downright vulgar, perfectly reflected the standards and whole hearted self confidence of the age. Surviving largely intact until the Second World War, this City finally fell to the bombs of the Blitz, and even more so to the wholesale redevelopments that started in the 1960s. Only now with so little remaining can we see what has been lost and appreciate the amazing variety of styles, the imagination and sheer exuberance of that period of design. The survivors of earlier periods are safe now, having reached that stage of their existence where great age alone is enough to ensure survival, but the products of the Victorian age have not yet reached this state of grace. They are still under threat, and it behoves us to appreciate and enjoy them while they yet remain.

The best time to see and 'feel' the City is on a Sunday when, apart from the main thoroughfares, the streets are clear of traffic and the silence is only broken by the sound of bells ringing out from St Paul's and St Mary le Bow and the cooing of the pigeons. The Underground Central Line is a useful artery, but the best way to travel is on foot, not so great a hardship as the area encompassed by the old Roman wall was surprisingly small.

We hope that you will find your journey of exploration an interesting and pleasant one, and that during your travels you will share some of the pleasure in the subject that inspired us to write this book.

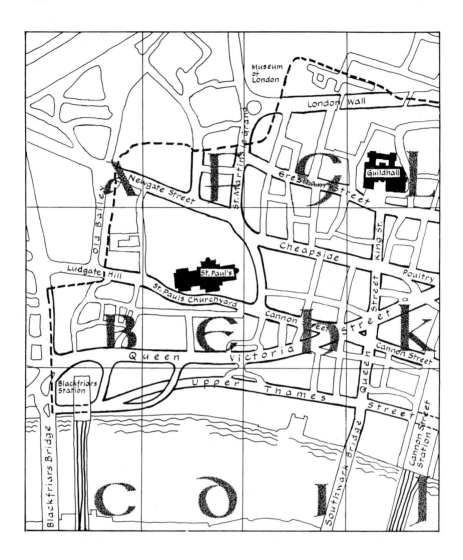

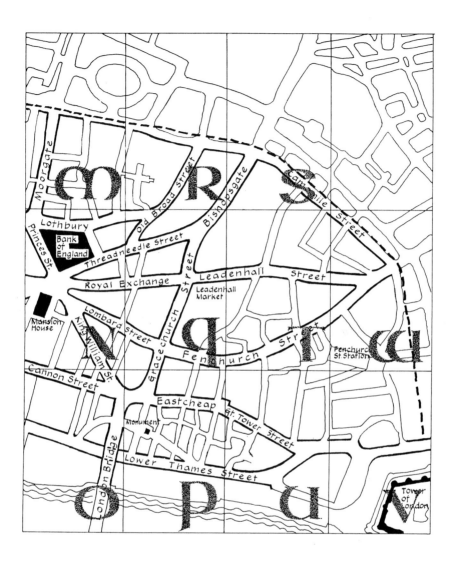

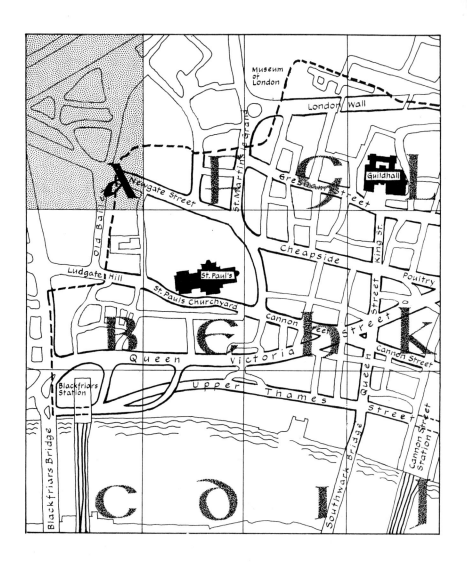

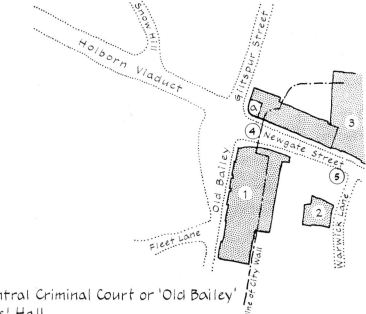

1 The Central Criminal Court or 'Old Bailey'
2 Cutlers' Hall
3 The General Post Office
4 Site of New Gate
5 Warwick plaque

a The Viaduct Tavern

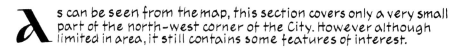

As can be seen from the map, this section covers only a very small part of the north-west corner of the City. However although limited in area, it still contains some features of interest.

Newgate Street, the main access to the City from Holborn, derives its name, as one might guess without too much difficulty, from New Gate, one of the five principal gates in the City Wall. The gate was sited a few yards east of the Viaduct Tavern public house on the corner with Giltspur Street, and was restored in 1672 following damage to the original in the Great Fire of 1666. This was the last time that substantial repairs were carried out on the Gate which had already been rebuilt in the early fifteenth century following extensive damage caused during an assault by Wat Tyler's mob in 1381. The Gate was also badly affected by fire in 1556, entailing more repairs.

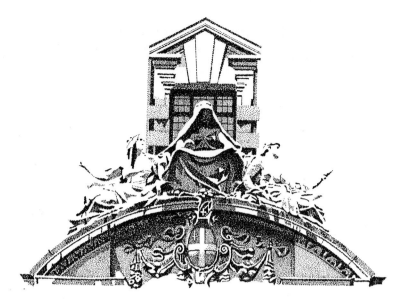

Entablature over the Old Bailey doorway

During its long history the Gate had the rather dubious distinction of doubling up as a prison, a tradition dating back at least as far as the reign of King John. The inmates were accommodated on the first floor above the entrance arch, in an atmosphere that one imagines could have been cut with a knife. To give an idea of how many could be housed in what must have been a relatively small space, it was recorded that fifty two inmates perished there in the Great Plague of 1665. No doubt too the gaol fever, a virulent form of typhus, carried off more prisoners than the hangman's noose.

The gateway was demolished in 1777, following an Act passed in 1760 for the removal of all of the City gates. Not that they served much purpose by then anyway, because most of the Wall had been systematically taken down during the previous fifty years.

And so the original fortified City was no more, a victim of the rapidly expanding population, and of building works in the London area which had commenced earlier in the century.

Anyway, back to the present, and that symbol of British justice, the Central Criminal Court or 'Old Bailey'. It was built between 1900 and 1907 to the design of E.W. Mountford in what might affectionately be described as 'neo English baroque, and is of a size and aspect guaranteed to reflect the austerity of its function.

A 3

With this in mind, note the impressive doorway, complete with somewhat sinister shrouded figure peering down from above. A sobering and not very optimistic sight for the accused passing through its portals. And then, of course, you have the most famous symbol of all above the dome, the figure of justice complete with scales and sword held aloft.

The Old Bailey, which superseded the Old Sessions House further down the road, was built on the site of Newgate Gaol, which had been designed by the City's architect, George Dance the Younger, and built between 1770 and 1778. Dance also rebuilt, at the same time as Newgate, the previous Sessions House which had survived since 1539.

Newgate Gaol was a very fine and powerfully designed building, and the pity is that it was chosen as the site for the Old Bailey. It was originally designed to accommodate 400 prisoners, cost £75,000 and was completed just in time to suffer considerable damage during the Gordon Riots in June 1778. A further £30,000 was needed to repair the damage. Although Lord George Gordon, the anti-Papist perpetrator, escaped punishment (which is more than a hundred and thirty-five of the more prominent rioters did) he nevertheless became an inmate of the gaol five years later, having been found guilty of libelling the French Queen, Marie Antoinette. He remained there until his death in 1793 from gaol fever.

In 1783 Newgate Gaol acquired a very popular attraction. It became the venue for public executions, following the transfer of this activity from Tyburn (where Marble Arch now stands). The debut for this spectacle occurred on the 3rd. December, when ten people were hanged at one sitting, if that's the right phrase! At Tyburn, though, things had been better organized for the spectator, a permanent viewing-stand having been provided which was known as 'Mother Proctor's Views'. A charge was made for the use of this facility. Greater attendances were expected if drawing and quartering formed a part of the sentence.

Anyway, back to Newgate, where, during one display, twenty-eight people were killed and seventy injured, when panic broke out in the crowd of nearly 40,000 on the 22nd. February 1807 during the hanging of Holloway and Haggerty. The last public execution, in which the victim was Michael Barrett, occurred in 1868.

Certainly the most infamous villain to have lived in the street known as the Old Bailey was Jonathan Wilde, thief-taker and handler of stolen goods, and king of the underworld in the early eighteenth century. Ironically his headquarters were situated only a few doors from the Sessions House. On the 24th. May 1725 he met the fate to which he had consigned so many being hanged on the Triple Tree gallows, one of at least fifty thousand to have been executed at Tyburn during the course of six centuries.

The north side of Newgate Street is occupied by a row of late Victorian offices with shops underneath and is a rare sight in the City these days, rare because it has so far escaped the ball and chain which has flattened so much else in recent years. So, although not of any special architectural interest it is worth a quick glance whilst it is still there. The row finishes with the Grade II listed (no guarantee against the bulldozer) GPO building that will be described in Area F.

As you turn from Newgate Street into Warwick Lane you will notice a small stone tablet let into the wall of a modern office building. This has obviously graced many a building on the site over the centuries, and features a figure in armour with the initials GC and the date 1668. It records the site nearby of the mansion of the Earls of Warwick, perhaps the most famous of whom was Richard Neville the notorious 'Kingmaker' of the Wars of the Roses who dwelt here with an army of 500 retainers. Obviously he was not a man to be trifled with. He died in the mists at the Battle of Barnet in 1471, to the relief of friend and foe alike.

Moving on down Warwick Lane we come, on the right, to Cutlers Hall, a simply but strongly modelled red brick and red stone building designed by T. Taylor Smith and built between 1886 and 1887. Apart from the pleasing proportions of the facade, another attraction is the terracotta frieze by Benjamin Creswick, a protege of Ruskin, which depicts men labouring at the various processes of converting raw material into the finished product.

Cutlers' Hall stands on the site of the College of Physicians, rebuilt after the Great Fire by Wren and completed in 1674. As an adjunct to those functions implied by its name, it also became, following an Act of Parliament in 1752 authorizing dissection, the end of the journey for many felons convicted of a capital offence. Having been tried at the Old Bailey Sessions House, with subsequent committal to Newgate, their route lay west through Holborn and Oxford Street to Tyburn. Following public execution, they were taken back to Warwick Lane to a fate of which by this time they were fortunately unaware.

We now move on and enter Area B.

Cutlers' Hall - Warwick Lane

A 6

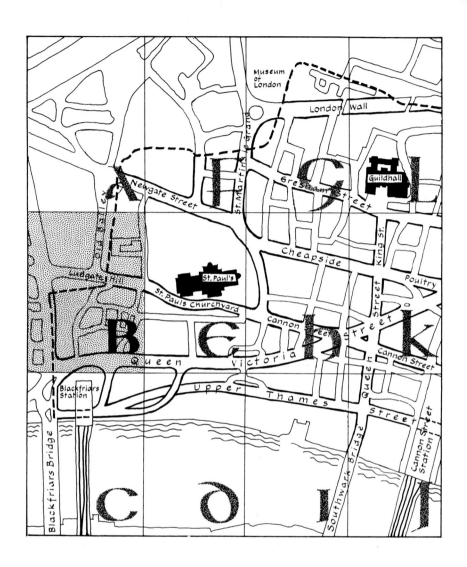

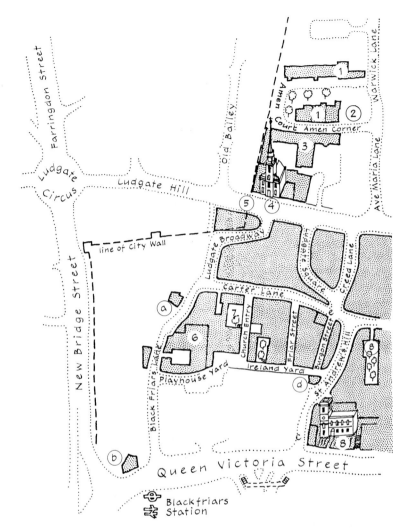

1   Amen Court
2   Amen Corner
3   Stationers' Hall
4   St Martin within Ludgate
5   Site of Lud Gate
6   Apothecaries' Hall
7   Churchyard of St Ann Blackfriar
8   Wardrobe Place

a   The Queen's Head
b   The Blackfriar
c   The Baynard Castle
d   The Cockpit
e   The Rising Sun

B   8

So, carrying on from Area A and continuing down the west side of Warwick Lane, we come to Warwick Square which, although now devoid of interest, would certainly have been worth a visit thirty or so years ago in order to see Amen House at its western end. This late seventeenth century house on three storeys was unfortunately demolished in recent years, and replaced with that which we see now, presumably to complete the development of the square.

To the south of Warwick Square we come to Amen Court, a Victorian complex, and beyond that, Amen Corner. This is a private thoroughfare and is referred to in Roque's map of 1746 as the 'Residences of St. Paul's Houses'. They still form part of the Cathedral Estate, being the canons' houses, and an appointment is needed before venturing into the Court. Numbers 1-3 date from the late seventeenth century and are now representative of a very few remaining examples of post-Great Fire rebuilding. At the western boundary at the back of the Court a small section of the original City wall is still visible. This comprises Roman first courses, some medieval masonry, and later brickwork over.

Abutting number 3 Amen Court and extending west and north across the square once stood the Oxford Arms coaching inn, demolished in 1877. This was originally approached from Warwick Lane via Oxford Arms Passage, on the same spot as the present northern entrance to Amen Court. The Oxford Arms belonged to the Dean and Chapter of St Paul's, and was rebuilt shortly after the Great Fire, still retaining the form of a galleried courtyard. Very evocative photographs of the building published in 1875 by the Society for Photographing Relics of Old London still exist, and a copy of the book can be seen in the Guildhall Library. The remainder of Amen Court dates from the 1880s, following demolition of both the Inn and the Oxford Arms Passage.

Ave Maria Lane, the continuation of Warwick Lane, sounds as though it should be interesting but isn't (although it probably once was), it does nonetheless provide access through concrete to a small square containing Stationers' Hall. This is, despite its relatively small scale, an unmistakably civic building of great charm. It was built in the late seventeenth century to replace its predecessor which perished in the Great Fire, although the basement walls are probably part of the pre-Fire building. In 1800 it was re-faced in stone by the Scottish architect Robert Mylne, in a style reminiscent of the Adam Brothers. Forty years earlier Mylne had won a competition, at the age of twenty-five, for rebuilding Blackfriars Bridge. Surprisingly this was only the second bridge to be built across the Thames along the City frontage in its long history. The bridge lasted roughly a hundred years before being replaced by the one we see today.

Stationers' Hall

The western boundary of Stationers' Hall virtually follows the line of the City wall, as does the church of St Martin, Ludgate. This was designed by Wren and built between 1677 and 1687 at a cost of £5,378; it is now the only pre-Victorian building left in Ludgate Hill.

Just to the west of St Martin stood another of the City gates, that of Lud Gate, the principal entrance to the City from the west via Fleet Street. The Gate was demolished in November 1760, having been sold to a certain Mr Blagden, a carpenter of Coleman Street, for £148.

Presumably he was then able to develop the land on either side of the road. From 1377 Ludgate doubled up as a debtors' prison, a function, like Newgate, maintained until its demolition.

In Ludgate Hill, two listed buildings, numbers 34-40, replaced smaller four storey buildings in the 1870s.

Nearly all of the buildings in Ludgate Broadway, Ludgate Square and Creed Lane have been built since the last war. Strangely enough, the one and only listed building in these streets, numbers 1-3 Ludgate Square, has recently been demolished.

As can be seen from the map, all roads lead to Carter Lane. In Horwood's map of 1792 this particular western section was called Shoe Makers Row, and it forms the backbone of several interesting streets running south, which we will explore shortly. Meanwhile, starting with Blackfriars Lane, we pass, on the right, the Queen's Head, a Victorian public house and now a Grade II listed building. It stands alone, a relic of a previous age. The site to the north is the last of the derelict war-damaged sites and is now being developed; the site to the south has been developed in recent years.

In the course of all this activity, two thoroughfares have been lost, Pilgrim Street and Apothecary Street, which connected Blackfriars Lane with New Bridge Street. Opposite what was Apothecary Street stands Apothecaries' Hall, founded on the site in the reign of James I by Gideon de Laune, apothecary to Anne of Denmark. Although a victim of the Great Fire, it was rebuilt in 1684, suffered alterations to the facade in 1779, and acquired a new door surround in the mid-Victorian era.

St Martin within Ludgate

Nevertheless the overall effect is still very pleasing, as is the internal courtyard, easily accessible from the street. The southern facade is bounded by Playhouse Yard, a reference to the site of a theatre founded there in the sixteenth century. The theatre was short-lived because of restrictive laws introduced by the civic authorities shortly afterwards: obviously theatre was not the right sort of activity to be encouraged within the confines of the City walls. So the theatre decamped and set off for Southwark. Shakespeare lived in Ireland Yard close by at this time, being both a partner in the venture and a regular theatre-goer.

An open space in Ireland Yard marks the site of the Tudor church of St Ann Blackfriars, destroyed in the Great Fire and not rebuilt thereafter.

Apothecaries' Hall - the courtyard

The church took over the site from the Great Dominican Priory of Blackfriars, a victim of the Reformation, dissolved in 1538.

Turning off Ireland Yard we come to Church Entry, a narrow passageway containing the churchyard of St Ann Blackfriars. This is marked by a small garden with occasional tombstones to denote its previous use. It is one of many such small havens within the City. Opposite this is St Ann's vestry hall, a very pleasantly proportioned brick and stone facade designed by Sir Banister Fletcher and Son and built in 1905. Roque's map of 1746 indicates that a tennis court existed just north of the vestry, an unusual facility for the City which had gone by 1792.

In Carter Lane, near the junction with Ludgate Broadway, is a tiny passageway called Carter Court, indicated on Roque's map as Fluor de Lis Court. The court itself, which is a small open space in a modern development, is approached through a passageway in number 81, Carter Lane, on one side of which can still be seen the original plaster lath behind the timber lining. The house is late seventeenth century and is a Grade II listed building.

Most of the buildings in Ludgate Broadway, and on the north side of Carter Lane as far as Friar Street, have been rebuilt in recent years in a manner sympathetic with their surroundings, showing a welcome attitude to design in such situations. At the junction of Carter Lane and Burgon Street is the Rising Sun public house, a Grade II listed Victorian building. It is well worth a visit, and is one of the few pubs open on a Sunday.

St Ann's Vestry Hall

Burgon Street, formerly New Street, still retains the character of a narrow Victorian street. The Pinnochio wine bar is situated on the west side. Turning from Burgon Street towards St Andrew's Hill, we pass, or perhaps call in at, the Cockpit public house, another Grade II listed building. The facade incorporates some very delicate and ornate stonework detail at frieze and cornice levels, and also illustrates how good the Victorians were a 'turning corners' with their buildings.

And now to St Andrew's Hill, one of the most appealing backwaters in the City. Numbers 31 and 36 are both good examples of mid-eighteenth century domestic architecture and both are listed. Numbers 31 and 32, in brickwork with stone dressings, curved to follow the street line, are scheduled for demolition and redevelopment at the time of writing. From both an architectural and street-scape point of view this must be one of the most sensitive areas left in the City, having escaped the monumental office boom building programme. It was declared a Conservation Area in 1971.

The church of St Andrew -by-the-Wardrobe, fully exposed when viewed from Queen Victoria Street, was rebuilt by Wren between 1685 and 1695 at a cost of £7,060. It was the only building in this area to be hit by enemy action during the last war, and restoration work to the gutted interior was carried out in the 1960s.

The Cockpit

St. Andrew's House

The tower and main facades escaped damage, but were remodelled to return them to Wren's original design, as will be apparent from the patchy brickwork left after the removal of the late Victorian stone banding and ornamental features.

A narrow alleyway, with many delightful corners and views, leads round the north side of the church and thence to Wardrobe Terrace via Wardrobe Chambers, an impressive Victorian stone and red brick office building. This can also be approached from Queen Victoria Street by steps at the side of St Andrew-by-the-Wardrobe. To the right of these steps, and also fronting Queen Victoria Street, is the imposing British and Foreign Bible Society building of 1869 by E. I'Anson. It is well worth a quick look.

Seeing that we are now in Queen Victorian Street, let's say a few words about it. It was created during the period 1867-71, to connect the newly-formed Embankment west of Blackfriars Bridge with the Bank of England in the heart of the City. The developments lining the thoroughfare became increasingly extravagant in style the closer they got to the Bank, ranging from arcaded Gothic to Italian Renaissance, and culminating in the Bucklersbury triangle housing the premises of Mappin and Webb. At the western end the route was closely associated with the wharves and warehouses of Upper Thames Street. After the last war, this usage having become redundant, the opportunity was taken to create more office space and widen Upper Thames Street to cater for the increase in motor traffic.

The only notable building left at the extreme western end is the Blackfriar public house on the corner with New Bridge Street.

St Andrew by the Wardrobe

This wonderfully ornate late-Victorian building, arts-and crafts mixed with art nouveau, now stands forlornly alone, all of its neighbours having been destroyed, not by enemy action but by post war redevelopment. The layered composition of the saloon bar entrance and windows over, complete with mosaic panel and adjoining decorative pilasters, is worthy of study in its own right. However, this is only a foretaste of the delights that lie within. Visitors are advised to investigate.

New Bridge Street, on the western end of the City limit as defined by the City wall, is of interest, as it follows the line of the old Fleet Ditch, a tributary which flowed into the Thames and served as an open sewage outfall at this point.

B 16

Access to the City was gained by crossing over the Fleet Bridge (whilst presumably holding one's nose), which was sited where Ludgate Circus now stands. This southerly exposed section of the 'Ditch' was covered over when New Bridge Street was created in conjunction with the construction of Blackfriars Bridge in the 1760s, there being no point in crossing the new bridge only to find oneself in deep water, or sewage! It is no wonder that typhus was so prevalent.

Wardrobe Place

Before moving away from the area covered by this section, the visitor should retrace his steps back up St Andrews Hill to Carter Lane, and from there into Wardrobe Place, one of the most secluded places in the City, and in total contrast to the concrete wasteland, the domain of the car, of Upper Thames Street. In character it is more reminiscent of a quiet corner in a small market town than a site in the City. All of the buildings on the western side are listed, including Wardrobe House at the southern end. Those on the eastern side are currently the subject of a Planning Application for demolition and redevelopment, so no doubt they will not be with us for much longer.

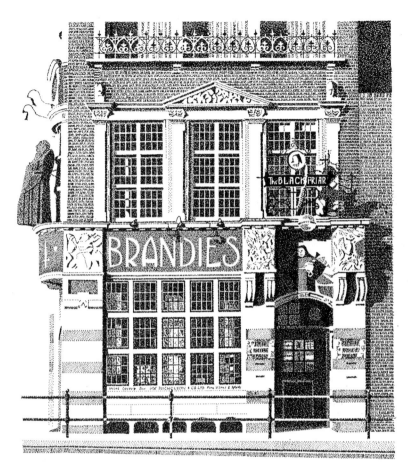

The Blackfriar

O f the listed buildings, numbers 3 – 5 date from around 1701. Wardrobe Place was built on the site of the Great Wardrobe, which moved from the Tower of London in the fourteenth century, and provided storage for royal garments used for state occasions. The original was destroyed in the Great Fire.

And now to Area C, about which I suspect there will be little to say.

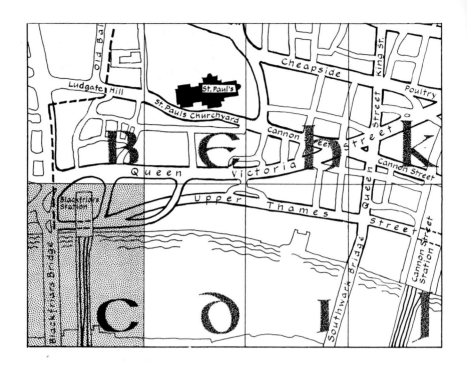

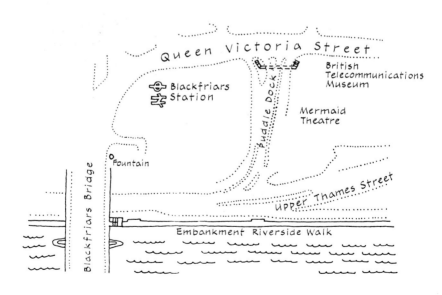

Yes, I was right. There is little to say except mention that perhaps the only worthwhile aspect of this area is the river side walk with views towards London Bridge, Tower Bridge and beyond what were docklands but are now mostly wastelands. Oh yes, and those seats with wonderful cast-iron camels are definitely worthy of closer inspection.

Twenty years ago this pedestrian route did not exist, as wharves fronted the riverside. However, these were swept away in the early 1970s with the creation of the Blackfriars underpass built on and above the Thames forshore and the widened Upper Thames Street.

In 1959 a theatre was again established in the City after an absence of almost four hundred years, namely the Mermaid of Puddle Dock. (All that's left of the Dock, now, are the puddles.) The theatre originally took the form of a smallish temporary-looking structure, which, during the construction of the roadworks aforementioned, looked rather like a large white pebble washed up on a beach of concrete. The theatre is now embedded in a modern office complex and is well signposted from Blackfriars Station.

As with this area, there may be little to say about Area D, so it is tempting to move on to Area E. But let's look just in case.

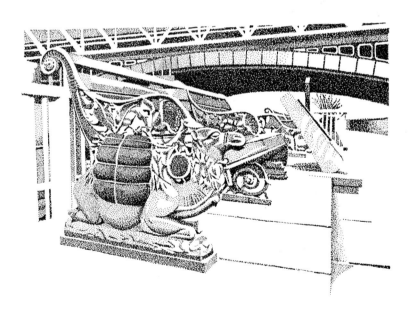

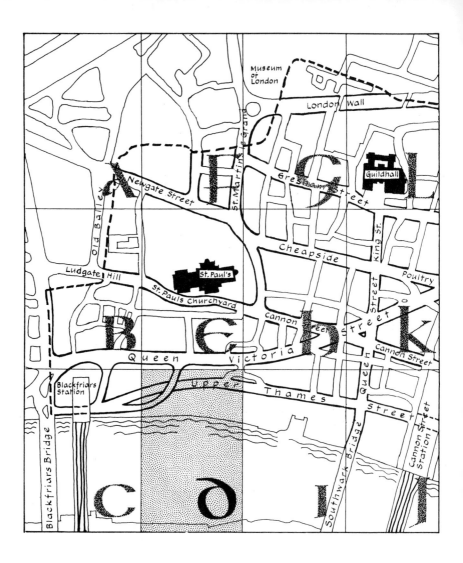

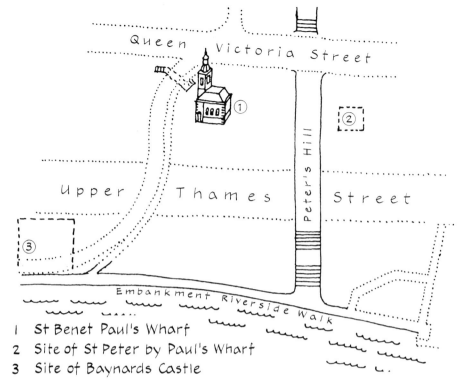

1 St Benet Paul's Wharf
2 Site of St Peter by Paul's Wharf
3 Site of Baynards Castle

bad you walked along the embankment into Area D before the Great Fire and glanced to your left, you would have found yourself looking at the river frontage of Baynards Castle. This particular version was the last in a line of castles bearing that name, the first having been built by Ralph Baynard, a Norman who came to England with the invasion of 1066. It remained in the hands of Norman barons until it was forfeited to the Crown in the reign of Henry I. Henry bestowed it on Robert Fitzgerald. Things remained relatively calm until the reign of King John, when the castle was demolished and then rebuilt with his permission by Robert Fitz-Walter. This castle lasted until 1428 when it was destroyed by fire. Fame followed when Richard III was offered the Crown there in 1483. Henry VII, his conqueror in battle two years later, used it as a royal residence. His son, Henry VIII, converted it from a castle to a palace. In 1553 Mary Tudor was proclaimed Queen there, and it remained a royal residence until falling victim to the Great Fire of 1666.

Anyway, rather than take the direct route to St Benet Paul's Wharf by skirting up White Lion Hill, not a very inviting prospect, why not instead continue along the embankment, enjoying the view, and thence to Peters Hill? The many steps bear witness to the name, and lead to a wide, soulless expanse of paving designed to give an uninterrupted view of St Paul's from the river. This view had been included, as being particularly desirable, in the 1944 report for post-war reconstruction in the City. The report also recommended the building of the race track that motorists know today, involving the acquisition and demolition of wharves along the river frontage. All in all, it was a rather prophetic document, finalised in the Corporation's 1962 Policy Plans. The decline of the centuries old Pool of London for shipping had already been envisaged at that stage. Anyway, this is just something to read about whilst you amble northwards to Queen Victoria Street.

Having arrived there, turn left and on to St Benet Paul's Wharf (the wharf disappeared in the road building works). It is hard to visualise now, but Upper Thames Street used to pass the south side of the church. Still, despite this, we do have the consolation of the riverside walk and views, which did not exist before.

On the opposite bank of the river can be seen a small group of period houses standing in splendid isolation against a backdrop of large industrial buildings. The white building at the left of the group is the house occupied by Wren whilst superintending the building of St Paul's.

And now to St Benet, designed by Wren, built by his master mason, Thomas Strong, and completed in 1683. As a design the church is truly individual, a lovely combination of plain brickwork relieved with stone quoins to the corners and garlands above the round-headed windows. It was one of only four churches to escape damage in the last war, but unfortunately suffered damage to its interior in the early 1970s due to vandalism. As you will see during your visit, this has been very well restored.

Now on to area E.

St Benet Paul's Wharf

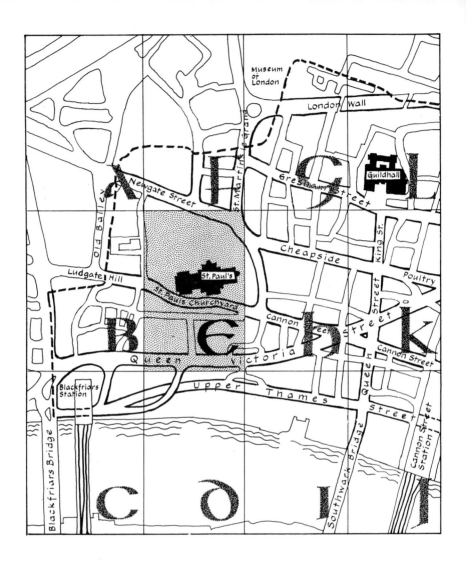

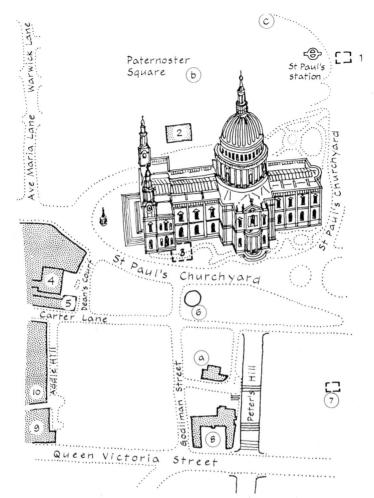

1 Site of St Michael-le-Querne
2 The Chapter House
3 Site of St Gregory
4 The Deanery
5 YHA
6 Information Centre
7 Site of St Mary Magdalen
8 College of Arms
9 British and Foreign Bible Society Building
10 The Bell

a The Horn Tavern
b The Sir Christopher Wren
c The Master Gunner

lancing across the street from St Benet the eye is drawn to a pair of sumptuously elaborate gates and screens fronting a courtyard containing the College of Arms, home of the Royal Heralds. The gate and railings, although dated 1956, are in fact much older and originated from Goodrich Court in Hertfordshire. The building itself has a strictly proportioned brickwork facade with imposing double curved steps and gallery, and was built between 1671 and 1677 by Morris Emmott. It was originally in the form of a quadrangle with inner courtyard approached through the west wing. The southern part of the quadrangle was sliced away in 1867, however, to make way for the laying out of Queen Victoria Street. The College of Arms was established on this site in 1555, having been given the late fifteenth century mansion of the Earls of Derby by Mary I. This building perished in the Great Fire.

The College of Arms - Queen Victoria Street

A s Godliman Street now contains nothing of interest (apart from the west side of the College of Arms) we might as well turn right and climb the steps of Peter's Hill towards St Paul's Cathedral, passing on the left the Horn Tavern public house. This was until recently an interesting little corner, but now progress has caught up with its surroundings. We come next to the City of London Information Centre, a circular, unmistakably 1950s building and well worth visiting to browse around and pick up leaflets and books, souvenirs and postcards.

Resisting the temptation to rush across the road to St Paul's, why not instead walk down Carter Lane to have a quick look at the recently renovated St Pauls Choir School building? Designed by F.C. Penrose and built in 1875 in the popular Romanesque style, it has now been converted to house the YHA's City of London hostel.

YHA City of London Hostel

The Bell – Addle Hill

Leading down from Carter Lane is Addle Hill, a narrow and gloomy street that has been frozen in time by planning blight. On the corner at the bottom of the hill is a derelict public house, the Bell, a typically Victorian hostellery where 'time' unfortunately was last called some years ago. Still adhering to the facade are war time air raid notices, which, if genuine, are testimony to the durability of contemporary adhesives!

And now to retrace our steps to the Choir School and the present.

The Deanery

Round the corner, in Dean's Court not surprisingly, stands the Deanery. It was designed by Wren and built in 1670, five years before work started on the new cathedral. What history this building has seen! Built at a time when most of the City was still trying to recover from the effects of the Great Fire only four years earlier, it sits serenely in its little tree filled courtyard, a million miles from the bustle of the City around it.

And now back to St Paul's, about which, as volumes have already been written, it seems prudent from a space point of view to say little. You are best advised simply to look around, both inside and out, and to venture from the depths of the crypt to the giddy heights of the whispering gallery and above, and, if further curiosity is aroused, return to the Information Centre.

However, we will mention that the first cathedral was built on this hill in 604 by the first Christian king in England, Ethelbert. This building lasted roughly seventy years before being replaced by one built in stone. This building was destroyed by the Vikings in 961, was rebuilt and destroyed by fire in 1087.

St Paul's Cathedral - doorway in north wall

It would be fascinating to know what the Saxon building looked like, it not having been influenced by the Normans. Anyway, the Normans got to work straight away to build cathedral number four, a structure by all accounts larger and higher than the present one. The nave survived over centuries of disasters and fires, as well as restorations, the last of which was undertaken by Inigo Jones in the early part of the seventeenth century. This restoration was very impressive, particularly the western portico, which Charles I paid for out of his own purse. In 1663 the 31 year-old Christopher Wren was appointed by the Dean and Chapter to advise on how best to effect repairs to the increasingly dilapidated building. It was by now in such a sorry state that Wren advised demolition and rebuilding. This suggestion was rejected, and so plans had to be drawn up for restoration, the report being presented only a few days before the Great Fire broke out on the 2nd. September 1666. There was a certain degree of disagreement about the designs presented by Wren, with the result that the building we see now, constructed between 1675 and 1711, was not his preferred concept.

St Paul's Chapter House

he gave the honour of laying the last stone in the lantern, in October 1708, to his son Christopher, who was born in the year work started on the cathedral.

St Paul's churchyard is worth strolling around, to note the early eighteenth century cast-iron railings and the rather uninspiring facade of the Chapter House, again by Wren and built between 1712 and 1714. It was gutted in the last war and has since been restored. And, of course, there is that mostly un-noticed feature of countless tourist photographs, the statue of Queen Anne which graces the west front of the cathedral. It is a stone copy of the marble original of 1711 by Francis Bird.

North of St Paul's we come to that endlessly controversial Paternoster Square development of the mid-1960s. It replaced a largely Victorian area, devastated in the war, which had been famous for centuries as the place where booksellers had their shops and publishers their headquarters. One hopes that the present wind-blown, bleak space will not be with us for much longer. However, every generation probably feels that they have the right solution to the development of such highly sensitive areas.

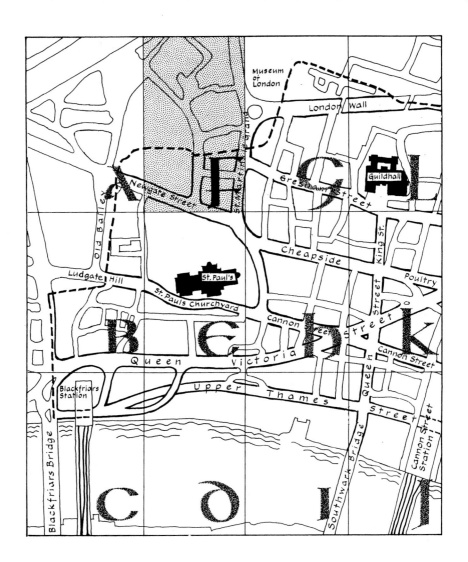

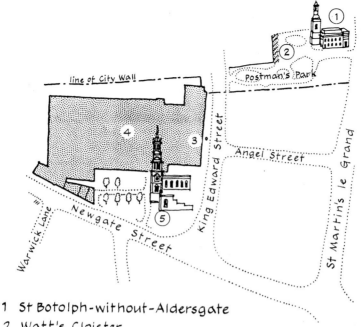

1 St Botolph-without-Aldersgate
2 Watt's Cloister
3 Sir Rowland Hill statue
4 General Post Office Building
5 Christchurch Newgate Street

Crossing the windy wasteland of Paternoster Square we arrive back in Newgate Street and return to the GPO building we mentioned in Area A. The complete building, which stretches from King Edward Street, pokes its nose out at its western end (the bit we see here) in the space previously occupied by the entrance forecourt of Christ's Hospital School, built in 1825 and designed by John Shaw. Christ's Hospital occupied the site since its establishment in 1552. Before that it was the turn of the Grey Friars monastery, a victim of the Reformation, which had been there since 1225. Anyway, the hospital decamped to Horsham in 1902, thus freeing the site for the present building, erected between 1905 and 1911 and now a Grade II listed building. The GPO at this time already occupied two large sites in St Martin's le Grand, both of which have now vanished, one in 1913 and the other in the 1960s.

Christchurch

Just beyond the GPO and adjoining buildings is the courtyard of Christ Church Newgate Street. The best way to approach what remains of the church is to enter the church yard and thence down the tree lined avenue towards the tower. In this way you can almost imagine that the church is still complete. The tower is almost as inventive and pleasing as that of St Mary-le-Bow. Fortunately it survived the bombing which gutted the interior of the body of the church. However, unlike some of the other City churches similarly affected, it was not restored. The reason for this was that the site had been earmarked in the City's 1962 Comprehensive Development Plan for road improvements. And so it came to pass that in 1974 the rear of the church was lopped off for a roadway realignment. A rather sad end for a church designed by Wren and built between 1677 and 1704. It was one of his most expensive : at £11,778 it was only a hundred pounds or so less than St Lawrence Jewry. The previous church, destroyed in the Great Fire, occupied exactly the same site as the conventual church of the Grey Friars monastery previously mentioned. The only reminder of this now is Grey Friars Passage, transversing the site in front of the tower.

Turning now into King Edward Street, we come to the main facade of the GPO building, which also houses the National Postal Museum, and what could be more appropriate than the statue of Sir Rowland Hill by the main entrance ?

Sir Rowland Hill

The statue is by Onslow Ford, dated 1881, and is a fitting memorial to the creator of the Penny Post which revolutionised the postal system when introduced in 1840. The building itself was loyally named King Edward's Building after the reigning monarch at the time that the building work commenced. It was constructed between 1905 and 1911 to the design of Sir Henry Tanner, although by 1911, however, George Ⅴ had been crowned. While on the subject of kings, this street is a relatively recent addition to the City, having been laid out in 1843 and named after Edward Ⅵ, who reigned between 1547 and 1553.

Although not actually within the original walled boundary of the City, Postman's Park is well worth a visit whilst on the way to Area G.

DAVID SELVES AGED 12.

OFF WOOLWICH SUPPORTED HIS DROWNING PLAYFELLOW AND SANK WITH HIM CLASPED IN HIS ARMS.

SEPTEMBER · 12 · 1886

WILI

LOST HIS IN SAVING THE A

FI

ERNEST BENNING COMPOSITOR · AGED 22 UPSET FROM A BOAT ONE DARK

inding our way along its well bordered path we come to a curious lean-to structure known as Watt's Cloister. It was erected 'In Commemoration of Heroic Self Sacrifice'. Within the shelter we find lines of faience tablets recording acts of great heroism by named individuals who lost their lives in the course of saving others. They start in the Victorian era with Sarah Smith, pantomime artist who died on the 24th. January 1863, and end with police constable Percy Cook, who died on the 7th. October 1927. The cloister was the gift of the great Victorian artist George Frederick Watts, and was opened by Sir William Richmond in 1899.

Continuing through the park we come to the church of St Botolph-without-Aldersgate, a charming brick building with a quaint spire, the whole a simple exercise in brickwork designed by Nathaniel Wright and built between 1788 and 1791.

St Botolph

The stuccoed elevation to Aldersgate Street is later, dating from 1831 and is very nicely proportioned, although slightly at odds with the modest design of the rest of the church. The Victorian drinking fountain and railings complete the picture and add a touch of domesticity. The church is the latest in a long line of buildings on the site stretching back to the thirteenth century.

Being careful to avoid the busy traffic whilst crossing the road, we come to the Lord Raglan and then Gresham Street and into Area G.

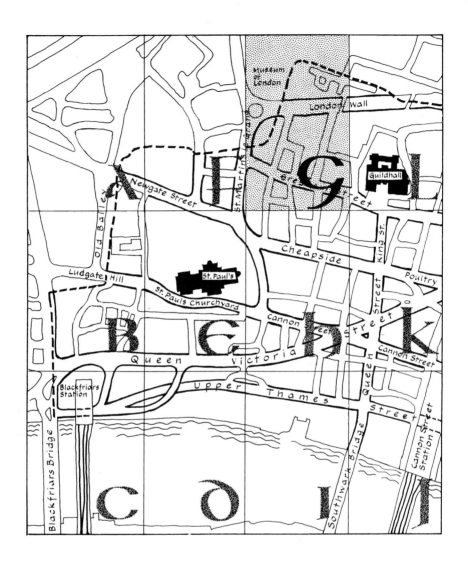

The map shows part of the City of London, including the following labels:

Museum of London, London Wall, Guildhall, Newgate Street, St. Martin's le Grand, Gresham Street, King St., Cheapside, Poultry, Old Bailey, Ludgate Hill, St. Paul's, St. Pauls Churchyard, Cannon Street, Queen Victoria Street, Queen Street, Cannon Street, Blackfriars Station, Upper Thames Street, Southwark Bridge, Cannon Street Station, Blackfriars Bridge

1 Site of Cripplegate
2 Barber Surgeons' Hall
3 City Wall bastion
4 Site of St Olave Silver Street
5 Remains of City Wall
6 St. Ann and St Agnes

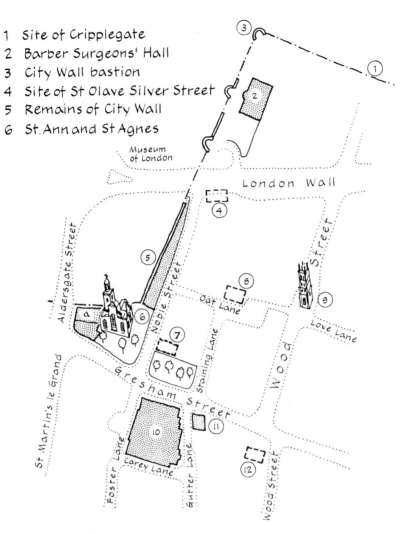

7 Site of St John Zachary
8 Site of St Mary Staining
9 Tower of St Alban Wood Street
10 Goldsmiths' Hall
11 Wax Chandlers' Hall
12 Site of St Michael Wood Street   a The Lord Raglan

And so to Gresham Street, once made up of St Ann's Lane, Maiden Lane, Lad Lane and, in the area of the Guildhall, Cateaton Lane. By the 1870s this had become simplified to St Ann's Lane and Gresham Street West leading to Gresham Street. Finally, by the end of the last century, to save further confusion, the whole had become simply Gresham Street. Thus for many years it had not been a particularly steady address for the receipt of mail!

An interesting little cluster of late-Victorian buildings mark the beginning of Gresham Street, and worthy of note is the powerful yet modest extravagance bestowed on the doorway of number 1, St Martins House, dated 1891. Incidentally, if you had happened to be on this spot in 1913, and had looked across the road, you would have observed the demolition of that strictly classical pile, the General Post Office building. It had been built in 1830 to the design of Sir Robert (who also designed the British Museum) Smirke, and would have seen much increased activity a decade later with the introduction of the Penny Post. But all is peaceful now, a feeling confirmed by the sight of the Lutheran church of St Ann and St Agnes, a little jewel set in a sylvan churchyard. The church, designed by Wren and built between 1676 and 1687, incorporated the original fourteenth century tower which had survived the Great Fire. For some reason the inside of the church seems larger than it would appear from the outside, possibly because the plan comprises a square within a vaulted square, the smaller square defined on its corners by Corinthian columns. A delightful space. The outside has, since the War, had the stucco of 1820 removed to reveal the original red brickwork, a great improvement.

St Martins House

St Ann and St Agnes

The Victorian stained-glass windows have also been replaced with plain glazing, again a reversion to the original design.

Before the Great Fire, Noble Street interrupted the continuation of Gresham Street, with the chuch of St John Zachary closing the vista. The church was not rebuilt after the Fire, and an area close to the site is now a public garden, the actual site being of course the road itself. Turning left into Noble Street, we come to the edge of an area that was completely devastated in the last war. The destruction revealed whole sections of the old City Wall and these are now set in a grassed area with illustrated guides at various vantage points.

On the corner of Oat Lane opposite, Scriveners' Hall once stood, again a victim of the Great Fire, as was the church of St Mary Staining next door, now the site of another small public garden. Next to this is Pewterers' Hall of 1960 by David Nye and Partners. Before the War these premises were situated in Lime Street.

Noble Street goes on to meet the realigned London Wall, which was opened in 1959 and which crosses what was once Falcon Square. The site of the church of St Olave Silver Street is now marked by a small garden adjacent to London Wall. Looking at it now, it is hard to believe that this area was once a quiet backwater with a lot of historical associations and, until the end of the last century, the site of domestic buildings that had escaped the Great Fire. It seems tragic that unique examples of such houses should have been demolished by the Victorians.

The next stage is to climb the steps and take the pedestrian bridge over London Wall, at which point it is hard not to notice the increasingly monumental nature of the office developments in view, of which the latest and largest is Alban Gate, designed by Terry Farrell. The beginnings of these particular forms of development came with the lifting of the 100 ft. height restriction in the late 1950s. This resulted in the building of the first tower blocks in 1960, starting with Moor House at a height of 221 ft. The first 'big un' on London Wall itself was St Alphage House by Maurice Saunders and Associates in 1961.

At this point you may wish to make a detour to the Museum of London which is nearby.

Glancing down from the walkway we see the continuation of the City Wall that we saw before in Noble Street. This can be reached by decending to pavement level and turning down the slip road. Once in the garden one can wander around and follow the remains of the wall, which leads past Barber Surgeons' Hall, a post-war building by K.Cross.

London Wall bastion

Incidentally, 250 years ago the barber surgeons were caused considerable consternation by the case of a certain William Duel. Having been left to hang at Tyburn for over twenty minutes, his body was brought to them for dissection. Inexplicably, and fortunately for him, he regained consciousness in the nick of time!

Beyond the hall is a lake bounding the Barbican housing development, and, by carefully negotiating the edge you can discern a further, almost complete bastion of the wall. Thus ancient and modern can be seen living cheek by jowl.

Returning through the gardens and crossing the pedestrian bridge, we arrive in Wood Street. Halfway down you will notice a solitary tower, all that remains of the church of St Alban, the body of the church having been destroyed in the last war. The body was the more interesting part, having been designed by Inigo Jones and built between 1633 and 1634, Wren designed the tower, which was built between 1682 and 1687, and also remodelled the interior, Jones's work having been damaged in the Great Fire. The interior was later 'improved' and an apsidal end added to the chancel in 1858 by the Victorian architect Sir George Gilbert Scott.

We can now cut through Oat Lane to Staining Lane and back to Gresham Street, opposite Goldsmiths' Hall. This building dates from 1835 and was designed by Philip Hardwick, who also designed the City Club, to be mentioned in Area R. The Goldsmiths are one of the twelve great livery companies, and were founded in 1327. On the opposite corner is Wax Chandlers' Hall, a post-war building which replaces the Victorian one destroyed in the War.

Turning right into Wood Street, we pass the site of the church of St Michael, sold in 1897 for commercial redevelopment. Thus, of the six churches existing in this area before the Great Fire, only one, St Ann and St Agnes, now remains.

And now, we move into Area H.

St Alban

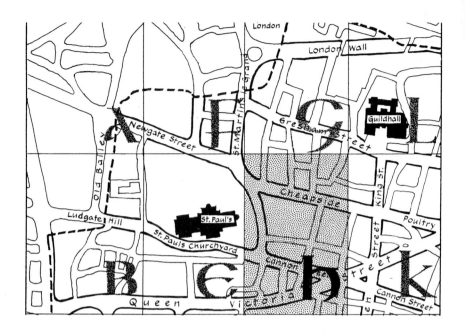

1 Site of the Collegiate Church of St Martin
2 Site of St Leonard
3 St Vedast
4 Site of St Peter Westcheap
5 Site of St Mary Magdalen Milk Street
6 Site of All Hallows Honey Lane
7 St Mary-le-Bow
8 Site of St Matthew Friday Street
9 Site of All Hallows Bread Street
10 Site of St John the Evangelist
11 Tower of St Augustine Watling Street
12 St Nicholas Cole Abbey
13 Site of St Margaret Moses
14 Site of St Mildred Bread Street
15 Site of Trinity Church
16 Painters' Hall
17 Site of St Nicholas Olave

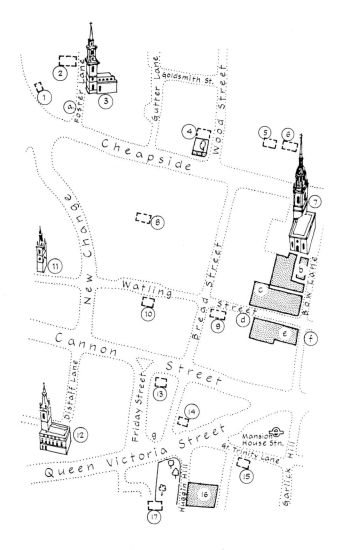

a   The City Pipe Wine bar
b   Bow Wine Vaults
c   Williamson's Tavern
d   The Red Lion
e   The Pavillion End
f   Ye Olde Watling
g   The Sea Horse

The east side of Foster Lane has a domesticity of scale that is quite appealing when compared with neighbouring streets, and leads well to the Wren church of St Vedast, built between 1670 and 1673 at a cost of £1,853. The tower and street elevations are, as with most Wren churches, faced with Portland stone. The church was gutted in the last war and the interior has been completely rebuilt. The treatment of the spire is rather unique in that, being a series of squares, it seem to grow from the tower, rather than being a separate structure stuck on as an afterthought. On Leake's map of 1667 the church on this site was noted as that of St Foster. A church on the opposite side of the road, St Leonard was burned down in the Great Fire and was not rebuilt.

Continuing down Foster Lane we come to Cheapside, a name derived from the Old English 'ceap' or market place. The earliest mention of the street, as 'Westcheap', was in the eleventh century, and as Cheapside in 1510. Looking at it now any historical associations are hard to imagine, apart from the sight of St Mary-le-Bow and a small cluster of buildings on the north side soon to be described.

However, looking down Gutter Lane one notices on the left hand side, surrounded by large modern blocks, what at first sight appears to be an old building but which was in fact built as recently as 1958. It was designed by L. Sylvester Sullivan in the 'imitation classical' style and houses the Saddlers' Company.

St Vedast

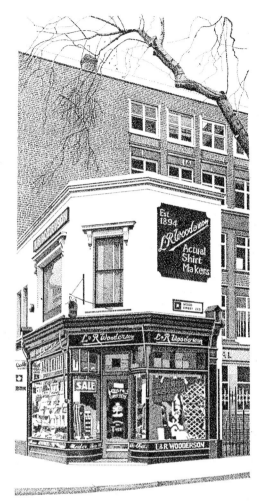

Further along Cheapside on the left is a delightful little cluster of shops, surviving both the War and later developments, including, on the corner with Wood Street, Wooderson's shirtmakers shop. This shop, sheltering under the umbrella of a large plane tree, is one of only a few in the City with a really pre-war feel about it. Next to this in Wood Street is the site of St Peter Westcheap, not rebuilt after the Fire. The railings are an interesting feature, and, if you enter what is now a small garden, you will notice a cast iron plaque, with apostles on the street side, and the inscription 'John Bradford Richard Garbrar Churchwarden 1712' on the garden side. Quite an unexpected little remnant in an area so comprehensively blitzed and redeveloped in the last fifty years.

Across the road, St Mary-le-Bow, probably the most famous church in the City, was a victim of the Blitz when the body of the church was burned out in 1940. Fortunately the tower and external walls survived relatively undamaged and the interior was restored and remodelled in the 1960s. It is worth visiting on a Sunday if only to hear the wonderful sound of the bells ringing out across the City, the famous 'Bow Bells' that traditionally conferred the title of Cockney upon those born within their sound. Hearing these one can imagine what a cacophony must have been created a couple of hundred years ago by the bells of over fifty churches in close proximity!

Moving round to the back of the church we come to Bow Churchyard leading to Bow Lane, a reminder of a time when such narrow passageways were a normal feature of the City. Fortunately the whole of Bow Lane escaped without damage in the War, evidenced by the mixture of domestic scale architectural styles dating from the mid-Victorian period onwards. On the left we come to a small passage named Groveland Court leading to Williamson's Tavern. The original building, called Williamson's Hotel, was built shortly after the Great Fire and played host to successive Lord Mayors until their official residence, the Mansion House, was completed in 1753. The present building dates from the 1930s, although the rather splendid wrought iron gates were presented to the original hotel by the monarchs William and Mary presumably between 1688 and 1694. The character of this little corner has been well maintained, and one hopes that it will remain so as it forms an intrinsic part of this unique little area.

Next door in Bow Lane, numbers 6-8 are listed buildings, built in 1874 in the brick, Venetian style popular with Victorian architects at this time. A small plaque appears on the next building, number 9, with St.MA (St. Mary Aldermary) and Ed. Carlisle/Richard Evans, Churchwardens 1865. On the opposite corner is Ye Olde Watling public house, a building dating from the early eighteenth century. The remaining houses on the west side were demolished in the late 1970s to make way for the present office development, unfortunate in its juxtaposition to the churchyard of St Mary Aldermary opposite.

One of the worst things to happen nearby in recent years has been the disappearance of Watling Court, an unspoilt early nineteenth century courtyard with the spires of St Mary Aldermary floating above the rooftops, and one of our favourite spots in the City. The Wren church of All Hallows Bread Street, on the corner with Watling Street, was sold in 1894 for commercial development.

Moving into Cannon Street, we head west and, walking past Bread Street, we come to a small open area, in front of a 1960s office block, with a commemorative tablet and bust over, which at first seems to represent Shakespeare but which is in fact of Arthur Philip, founder and first governor of Australia. The inscription and illustrations make interesting reading. The tablet was salvaged from the remains of St Mildred Bread Street followings its destruction in 1941. The church stood on the site of that (I can't find the right words to describe it!) Credit Lyonnais building opposite.

Continuing along Cannon Street to New Change, the visitor will notice a stone tower with graceful lead spire, obviously once part of a church but now with a strange appendage in tow consisting of heavy lead vertical cladding weighing down plain stone slabs below. This bizarre structure, the new choir school, replaced the Wren church of St Augustine Old Change, the body of which was destroyed in the War. Built between 1680 and 1687, it was very small, being only fifteen metres square including the tower and, unusually it had stained glass skylights in the vaulted roof.

Crossing the road and making our way down Distaff Lane we come to the church of St Nicholas Cole Abbey, again by Wren and built between 1671 and 1681. The church was burnt out during the War and presented a very sorry picture as late as 1962. However, it has been restored, including the trumpet shaped lead spire.

St Mary-le-Bow

Fortunately some internal features did survive, including the font cover, reredos, pulpit, and communion rail.

We now find ourselves back in Queen Victoria Street opposite the Salvation Army headquarters built in 1962 on an area that was flattened during the War. Crossing over to the building and continuing eastwards along the street we pass a sunken garden and proceed down Huggin Hill. Turning left along Huggin Court we come to Little Trinity Lane and Painter-Stainers' Hall, rebuilt after the Great Fire and again in 1916, only to suffer extensive damage again in the last War. The elevations we see, however, were not damaged, and so it remains an attractive building in a street otherwise bereft of interest.

And this I think concludes our tour of Area H, and so on to Area I, our visit to which may well be rather fleeting.

Williamson's Tavern

St Augustine (with big brother)

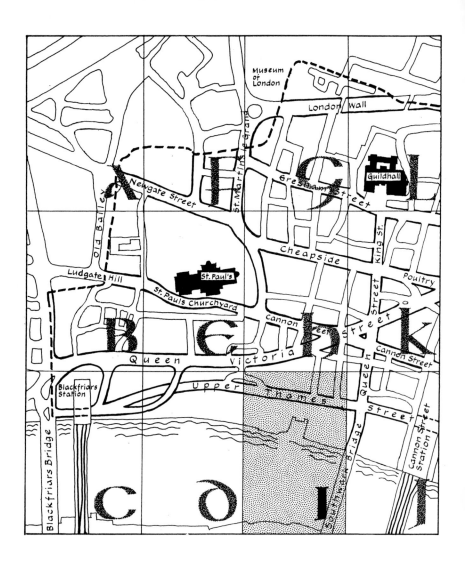

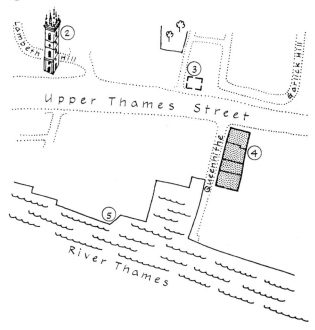

1   Site of St Mary Mounthaw
2   Tower of St Mary Somerset
3   Site of St Michael Queenhithe
4   Remaining wharf buildings
5   Broken Wharf

Brook's Wharf

Retracing our steps down Huggin Court and thence down Huggin Hill we reach the dreaded Upper Thames Street. If you were on the corner here in 1876 and had glanced to your left you would have witnessed the demolition of a splendid Wren church, St Michael Queenhithe. Somewhat similar in shape to St Benet Paul's Wharf, it was built of Portland stone rather than brick. The site was sold in 1876 and all that remains of the church is the weather-vane, comprising a ship in full sail, which now graces the spire of St Nicholas Cole Abbey recently visited in Area H.

And now for a rare sight, a glimpse of all that are left of the buildings that were once so typical of this part of the City. Opposite, in Queenhithe, is an all too short row of Victorian wharf buildings, two of which, numbers 20 and 21 are listed buildings. Although they are of no special architectural merit, they do nonetheless recall the days when the City, and the Upper Pool, were the centre of a thriving, worldwide, sea borne trade. They now stand alone and forlorn amidst the structures of another age and another type of commerce. Immediately adjacent is one of the few original access points to the river, which, leading to a small dock, gives one a view of the last remaining commercial riverside building in this area, the now derelict Brook's Wharf.

Returning to Upper Thames Street another incongruous object comes into view. Isolated in an alien townscape and imprisoned by motorway railings, stands the tower of St Mary Somerset. Seemingly a casualty of war, this remnant of yet another Wren church is in fact evidence of an earlier wave of commercial development. It was built between 1686 and 1694 and must have been an impressive building as it cost almost four times as much as St Vedast Foster Lane.

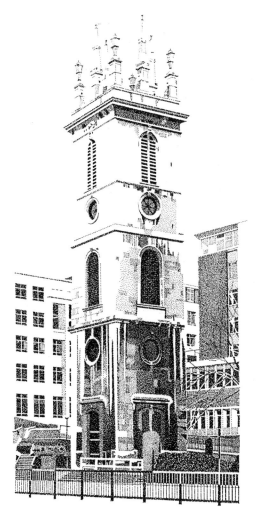

St Mary Somerset

The body of the church was demolished in 1871 to make way for the aforementioned commercial development, but fortunately the tower with its magnificent crown of obelisks was spared. It remains as a testament to the fertile imagination of Sir Christopher Wren in the ingenuity and diversity of his architectural solutions to the problem of interpreting an essentially medieval concept, that of the church tower, with or without spire, in the new, fashionable baroque style.

And now, crossing Upper Thames Street with care, we enter Area J.

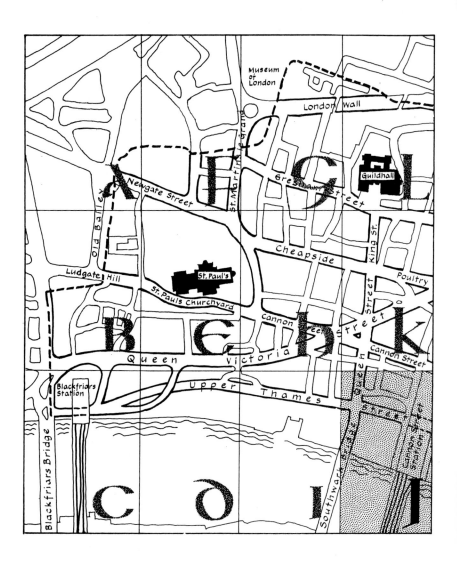

Museum of London

London Wall

G

Guildhall

Gresham Street

Newgate Street

St. Martins le grand

King St.

Cheapside

Poultry

Old Bailey

Ludgate Hill

St. Paul's

St. Pauls Churchyard

B E h K

Cannon Street

Queen Victoria Street

Cannon Street

Queen Street

Blackfriars Station

Upper Thames

Blackfriars Bridge

C O I

Southwark Bridge

Queen Street

Cannon Street Station

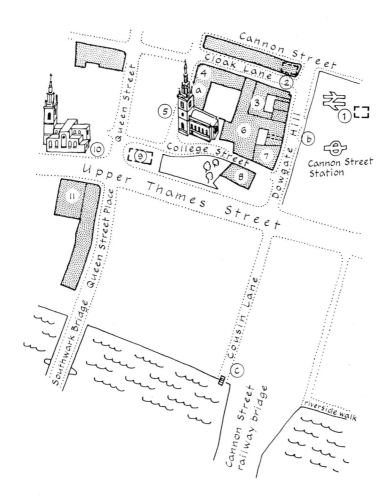

1	Site of St Mary Bothaw	7	Dyers' Hall
2	Site of St John Baptist	8	Innholders' Hall
3	Tallow Chandlers' Hall	9	Site of St Martin Vintry
4	College Hill Chambers	10	St James Garlickhythe
5	St Michael Paternoster Royal	11	Vintners' Hall
6	Skinners' Hall		

a	Whittingtons
b	The Bell
c	The Banker

The first building we come to in Upper Thames Street, a not very pedestrian-friendly thoroughfare, is the church of St James Garlickhythe. This has survived intact (well, almost) since being built between 1674 and 1687, with the spire being added between 1713 and 1717. It is curious to note that most of Wren's churches had spires added at a later date, suggesting they were afterthoughts, and they are not always totally in keeping with the tower below. The church, built to the same plan as its predecessor, destroyed in the Great Fire, is sometimes referred to as 'Wren's lantern' for the quality and intensity of the light that streams through the many lofty windows. Its unspoilt record ended in 1991 when a crane, being used on a nearby building site, crashed through the roof, causing untold damage. Repair work was still going on a year later. Before Upper Thames Street was widened in the early 1970's, the southern side of the church was fronted by domestic scale buildings mostly associated with the fur trade. Now that the elevation has been exposed we see the church in a way that was never envisaged by Wren constrained as he always was by the restrictions of cramped sites and existing buildings.

On the other side of the road, almost opposite, is an imposing stone building which is a lot older than it looks at first glance. Designed by Edward Jarman and built in 1671, Vintners' Hall, although altered during the Victorian era and again before the First World War, was finally restored to its original condition in the late 1940s. It is now a Grade I listed building, so should now remain sacrosanct. Next door, on the corner, is the Grade II listed Five Kings House of 1911, designed by Colcutt and Hamp. Note the rather attractive corner doorway, complete with naked couple perched on the pediment, overseen by cherubs from above, a small foretaste of the wonderful statuary to be seen round the corner on the Queen Street Place facade.

Continuing to the corner, we come to Queen Street, a relatively recent thoroughfare created after the Great Fire and named after Charles II's queen, Catherine of Braganza. The road formed part of a scheme to link London Bridge with the Guildhall. Crossing the road, and remaining in Upper Thames Street, we come first to the site of St Martin Vintry, not rebuilt after the Fire. Next is Whittington Green, a pleasant space named after that most famous of lord mayors, Dick Whittington, who founded a college nearby in, strangely enough, the road called College Hill.

The church of St Michael Paternoster Royal, designed by Wren and built between 1670 and 1677, was one of the first to be rebuilt after the Great Fire. The original church, St Michael in Elbow Lane, was the burial place of Dick Whittington, of which a little more later.

Continuing along College Street, we approach a cluster of City companies' halls, starting on the right with the Innholders'. Their building was completed in 1670 and, despite appearances, the street frontage was rebuilt in 1886 to the design of J. Douglas Matthews.

Fortunately the lovely early eighteenth century doorway was retained, complete with scrolled pediment and cascading garlands adorning each side of the doorway.

Reaching the corner with Dowgate Hill we come to Dyers' Hall, of 1839 -1840, designed by Charles Dyer (no relation). It consists of a strictly proportioned classical facade with liberal use of stone and brick work. All in all a rather pleasing effect. Next to this is Skinners' Hall, basically a late seventeenth century building with a street frontage designed by William Jupp a hundred years later. This consists of stucco with strongly modelled pilasters supporting an ornate pediment modelled by John Bacon in 1770. More impressive is the inner courtyard doorway, approached through a passage from the street, which dates from 1670. If this is a taste of the original building, one wonders why the street elevation was rebuilt.

The building adjacent, which incorporates an entrance door to Tallow Chandlers' Hall, dates from 1880, although the ground floor would appear to be relatively recent. Certainly the overhanging corner is very impressive. Of the four City Companies here, the Skinners' is the only one which is also one of the twelve Great Livery companies. The corner leads nicely into Cloak Lane, with a strangely blank elevation (narrow buildings used to abut it) and a rather appealing doorway to Tallow Chandlers' Hall in a small area with railings which occurs adjacent.

St Michael Paternoster Royal

Opposite this on the other side of the road and recessed into the building is an interesting memorial of 1884 recording the destruction of the churchyard of St John the Baptist, necessitated by the building of the District Railway. You will notice that the sound of the trains passing below is quite audible when standing and reading the inscription. Coming back to the other side of the road, the remaining half comprises a beautifully consistent red brick and stone terrace, of late-Victorian origin, named College Hill Chambers, enhanced by the doorway treatment with bay windows over. This small area repays a few moments just standing and staring before moving round the corner into College Hill. The first building completes the Cloak Lane terrace, and the doorway is of very similar design to its counterpart.

Next door, number 22, is an absolute gem, dating from the late seventeenth century. This is a real work of art with its two imposing pediments over the doorways, supported on volute corbels with garland decorations to infill the pediments, a theme continued around the circular windows over, the whole iced with Portland Stone. And how well St Michael looks when framed by such a street! What a comparison with the tower of St Mary Somerset and its backdrop of modern development!

Innholders' Hall

Number 33 opposite has a beautifully carved broken pediment over the doorway and surround, again supported on carved volutes framing a quite realistically carved face staring out across the street. Numbers 20 and 21 are early-nineteenth century, and number 20 occupies the site that once belonged to Dick Whittington's mansion. Dick Whittington, four times Lord Mayor (one short and three full-length terms) and three times buried, first by his executors, secondly in the reign of Edward $\overline{VI}$ when his treasures were thought to have been buried with him, and finally in the reign of Mary I, when his coffin was re-leaded.

To continue our tour of the block we continue down College Hill, past St Michael, turn right and thence back to Queen Street. This leads us north towards Area K, past the somewhat seedy but interesting-looking Victorian buildings on the other side of the road, which may not be around for much longer.

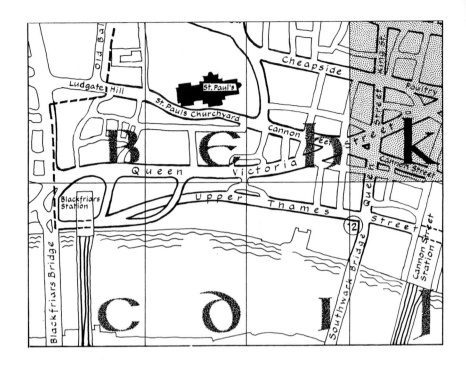

1	Remains of St Olave Jewry	a	The City Tavern
2	Site of St Martin in Ironmonger	b	The Magogs
3	Mercers' Hall	c	The Shades
4	Site of St Mary Colechurch	d	The Green Man
5	Mappin and Webb building	e	The Golden Fleece
6	Site of St Benet Sherehog	f	Mowbrays Wine Bar
7	Site of St Pancras	g	The Sugar Loaf
8	Site of St Antholin	h	The Hatchet
9	St Mary Aldermary	i	The Cannon
10	Albert Buildings	j	The London Stone
11	27-28 Queen Street		
12	Site of St Thomas the Apostle		

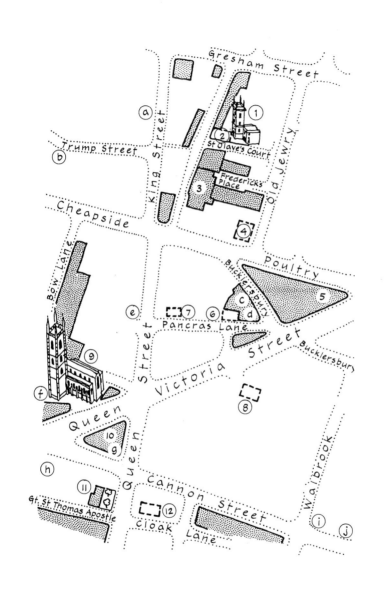

Gresham Street

ⓐ

Trump Street

ⓑ

King Street

St Olave's Court

①
②

Fredericks Place

③

④

Old Jewry

Cheapside

Bow Lane

Poultry

Bucklersbury

⑤

ⓔ

⑦

⑥

c

d

Pancras Lane

⑨

Bucklersbury

Street

ⓕ

Victoria Street

⑧

Queen

⑩

g

ⓗ

Queen Street

Cannon Street

Walbrook

⑪

Gt. St Thomas Apostle

⑫

Cloak Lane

ⓘ

ⓙ

K 64

The first small section of this walk, up to Cannon Street, escaped the Blitz and has so far remained undeveloped. Great St Thomas Apostle, although derelict (plants grow on the facades in many places) would look very well if restored. The varied buildings could provide a sparkling reminder of how a narrow Victorian Street could look in its prime. If only the City Council had a working conservation policy which extended further than public monuments and select small areas! Next door we come to numbers 27 and 28 Queen Street, a pair of what were once very fine eighteenth century houses until, unbelievably, the facades were painted in the late 1970s. Would you credit that this was allowed to happen? Two outstanding buildings ruined forever.

The large block bounded by Queen Street, Queen Victoria Street, Walbrook and Cannon Street used to be bisected by the continuation of Watling Street and Budge Row. However, the northern half was flattened by enemy action and the southern half, which survived, has since been redeveloped. From the ashes of the former has risen Bucklersbury House, now housing the Legal and General Building Society, which plays host to the Temple of Mithras in its forecourt. The Temple was discovered during excavations in 1954, and was a star attraction, being visited by 100,000 sightseers in five days in that year. The question is, in its present context of manicured granite and paving stones, does it look like a Roman relic of great importance? I leave that question with the reader. But who was Mithras? And why a temple to him? The cult of Mithras came originally from middle-eastern mythology and was adopted by the Romans in the first century BC. Women were excluded, and worshippers tended to be high-ranking soldiers and businessmen. The temples were both small and few in number, only five sites having been discovered in Britain so far.

The site of this temple was more recently occupied by the Wren church of St Antholin, which was unfortunately sold for the redevelopment of the site in 1874. The area south of Watling Street which survived the Blitz, was demolished and redeveloped anyway.

Fortunately, one of our favourite buildings, which marks the beginning of Cannon Street at the junction of Queen Victoria Street, has survived. This is the wonderfully exuberant arcaded Venetian gothic-style building by F. Ward of 1871. Opposite are two more on a smaller scale and of similar vintage fronting St Mary Aldermary. This church, older than them all, sits majestically behind, having witnessed many changes since its reconstruction by Wren. A condition of the bequest for the rebuilding of the church was that it had to be a copy of the old building, which had mostly been destroyed in the Great Fire. Certainly the tower is quite unique, the upper sections being built on the original in 1701-04.

So now for the remainder of Queen Victoria Street, leading towards the Bank and the area commonly known as the Bucklersbury triangle. The interesting buildings start at the junction with Sise Lane which is another good example of an inventive use of a corner junction followed by a main street facade treated in the grand manner.

Crossing over the road we get the full impact of the power-ful handling of the three-way junction with Pancras Lane and Bucklersbury. All are Grade II listed buildings. Notice also the splendid gothic-style doorway with decorative ironwork hinges to the oak doors of Mansion House Buildings. The door surround boasts pinnacles, peering heads and a coat of arms. Unfortunately this whole block, with its incredibly varied facades on the Poultry side, has been the subject of considerable planning controversy for many years, and permission was finally granted for demolition and redevelopment under the James Stirling scheme. Consequently the buildings have been allowed to go to ruin, appearing grimy and crumbling, with patterns of the asphaltic paint used on cracks in the facade. Imagine though what it could look like if a miracle happened and all three blocks were lovingly restored. One can but dream.

After returning across the road, it is worth spending a little time just ambling around the block. Whilst doing this, we stumble across the site of the pre-Fire church of St Benet Sherehog in Pancras Lane, with wall and railings erected in 1892, now looking rather gloomy in the shadow of the Victorian buildings in Bucklersbury.

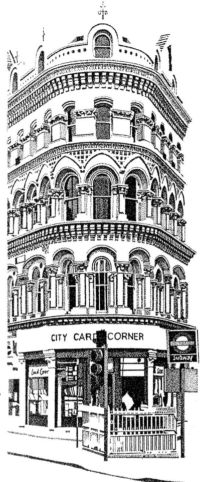

Moving on now, we must mention Sir Edwin Lutyen's Midland Bank on the north side of Poultry. This building, completed in 1939, is the pre-war counterpart of the solid, respectable and prestigious commercial idiom which had its roots in the early-Victorian period. However, not many match the appeal of Lutyen's work, which has the justifiably elevated status of a Grade I listed building, as have the Mansion House and Bank of England nearby. Adjacent to the Midland Bank is Grocers' Hall Court leading to Grocers' Hall. Rebuilt after the Great Fire, it had gardens fronting Prince's Street which lasted until the Hall was rebuilt in 1889-93 by H. Cowell Boys. A small part of this red brick and stone building still survives, now approached from the northern end of Prince's Street.

Albert Buildings

Moving westwards along Poultry we come to Old Jewry with, on the corner, the site of St Mary Colechurch, yet another church not rebuilt after the Fire. Now we come to Frederick's Place, a little enclave of houses built in 1776, but now with two exceptions. One is the building at the north-east corner, built in 1955 and doing its best to fit in with its surroundings. The other, at the end of Frederick's Place, is the rear elevation of Mercers' Hall which sports a small cluster of ward boundary marks. In an area so redeveloped, it comes as rather a surprise to find such an intact little cul-de-sac, and one can almost imagine Benjamin Disraeli turning the corner in the 1820s on his way to number 6.

Another notable person to have trodden these streets many centuries earlier was St Thomas à Becket, and a tablet in the wall of the Scottish Life building in Old Jewry commemorates the fact that he was born in a house nearby.

We now turn the corner into the delightful little passageway of St Olave's Court, home of the church of St Olave Jewry that was. The tower remains, a relic of the church designed by Wren and built between 1670 and 1679. The body of the church was demolished in 1888 for the usual commercial reasons . In the course of demolition it was decided to retain the west front. This gives the impression, when viewed from Ironmonger Lane, that the church still exists, and the whole effect, including the garden approach, is very pleasing. While mentioning the garden, it is worth noting that this was also the site of St Martin Pomeroy, or Ironmonger, destroyed in the Great Fire and not rebuilt. Also pleasing is the red brick and stone post-war building which flanks the south side of the passage.

What of Ironmonger Lane itself? Well, the character has been well maintained, and it is a pleasure to walk down. All the buildings are domestic in scale, in either brickwork or stone. Mercers' Hall, towards the southern end, looks as though it would benefit from a good clean up to bring out the interest of the stone facade.

On reaching Cheapside, we come to Atlas House, which is distinctive amongst City buildings by reason of its mini colonnade, an unusual feature, and because of its isolation, very noticeable. Turning into King Street we see a portrayal of Atlas, supporting the globe, crouching on an embellished keystone over the entrance. The building was designed by Thomas Hopper and built in 1836.

St Olave Jewry

King Street, like Queen Street, was a thoroughfare created after the Great Fire, and forms the northernmost section of roadways now connecting Southwark Bridge with the Guildhall.

The only other building of note in King Street is on the corner with Gresham Street. This is the Banca Commerciale Italiana, a Grade II listed building of 1850 by the architect Sancton Wood and one that fits its title quite well, having a pronounced continental look about it. Number 50 Gresham Street is occupied by Messrs Thresher and Glenny, Gentlemen's Outfitters, fittingly conservative, and an unlooked-for facility in the area.

And so, being in Gresham Street, we have reached the end of Area K and the beginning of Area L, leading us into Guildhall country.

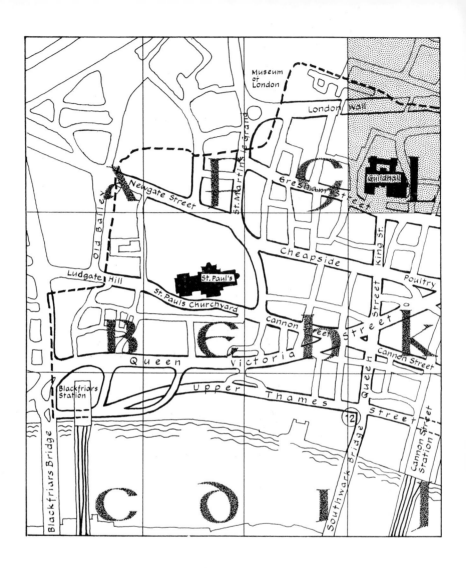

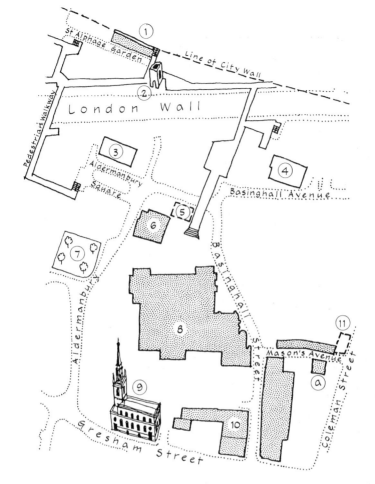

1   Remains of the City wall
2   Remains of St Alphage
3   Brewers' Hall
4   Girdlers' Hall
5   Site of St Michael Bassishaw
6   Chartered Insurance Institute
7   Site of St Mary Aldermanbury
8   The Guildhall
9   St Lawrence Jewry
10 Mayor's and City of London Court
11 Site of St Stephen Coleman Street
a   The Old Dr Butlers Head

Despite appearances, the Banco di Roma in Gresham Street, opposite King Street, is in fact a new building which would have been more in keeping with its surroundings 200 years ago. Still, it does respond to the historical nature of the area, more than the post-war effort further west on the other side of the road. Next we come to the Bank of New Zealand, a strongly modelled building with giant classical elements, built in 1912, with a splendid doorway round the corner in Basinghall Street. It stands on the site of the first telephone exchange to be built in Europe, in 1879, at 36 Coleman Street. Opposite this is Princes House by Robert Ansell and Curtis, a very solid commercial City building of inter-war vintage.

On the other hand, the building on our left, the Mayor's and City of London Court, of 1887 by Andrew Murray, seems to be an attempt to spread the idiom of the Guildhall itself into the surrounding streets. Of rusticated stonework, it is a classic example of 'Victorian perpendicular' style. This theme is taken up again with the Old Guildhall Library of 1873 by Sir Horace Jones, and a lot of thought must have gone into how best to handle the set-backs in the facade so as to follow the curve of the street.

On the other side of the road stands Bartlett House, a building of 1923 by Delissa Joseph, nicely proportioned and with a lightness of touch in the detailing. The one next to this is not unsurprisingly a Grade II listed building, namely numbers 13-14 Library Chambers of c.1875. This is in gothic style in red brick with Portland stone dressings. The corner of this leads into Mason's Avenue, the term 'avenue' being rather misleading in this instance. And what price the shock of seeing the mock-Elizabethan facade that stretches virtually the whole length of the northern side! The building was designed by T. Shearer, and the hopper heads are dated 1930. The temptation to try and revive the effect of a narrow medieval passageway must have been quite strong. A shame, though, about the recent polished granite and glass high level bridge connection from the building on the right, which rather detracts from the original effect. However, the Old Dr Butlers Head public house is a quaint and welcome survivor and rounds off the alley, sorry 'avenue', nicely.

Retracing our steps and turning left back into Basinghall Street we come, on the right, to Guildhall Yard, into which the Mayor's and City of London Court extends. At the end of this is a small and rather attractive house of c.1825, with stonework to the ground floor and yellow stock bricks above. The corner also contains Blackwell House, late-Victorian, and all stone. It takes its name from Blackwell Hall, previously Bakewell Hall, built on the site of a medieval cloth market. Blackwell Hall, rebuilt after the Great Fire, survived until its demolition in 1820. Finally, the corner with Gresham Street was rounded off with the Guildhall Tavern which lasted until the early part of this century.

St Lawrence Jewry, by Wren, built between 1670 and 1687 was, despite outward appearances, a victim of the Blitz when the interior was destroyed.

This has subsequently been restored by Cecil Brown. As regards the church itself, the spire sits rather awkwardly on the tower, which is not square, whereas the spire is, the reason being that the west front is not square with the body of the church. The church originally cost £11,870 to build, thus making it the most expensive of Wren's churches in the City, but then of course it is sited next to the Guildhall. The east elevation looks rather at odds with the south, being a scaled-down classical design with Corinthian pilasters and pediment dominated by a slightly higher parapet, the whole looking definitely out of scale and stuck on. The reference to Jewry reminds us that this area was the Jewish quarter of the City prior to their expulsion in the reign of Edward I.

As for the Guildhall itself, it is now slightly more visible than at the turn of the century, when it was hemmed in by buildings flanking the entrance and extending into the Yard. Even now, one can't help thinking that it would look better without the garish red and white entrance awning. First built in the early fifteenth century by John Croxton, a large proportion of the original stonework from the original hall still survives. The bulging Portland stone entrance, with elaborate pinnacles trying to outdo the rest, is by George Dance the Younger and dates from 1788-9. The building was severely damaged in the Great Fire, and, in the subsequent restoration, the walls were increased in height by approximately 20ft. This was rectified by Sir Horace Jones in 1865, when he reduced them to their original height and rebuilt the roof at the same time. Continuing our walk around the corner and past the little pond we arrive in Aldermanbury, and proceed northwards alongside the new extension until we reach the back of the building and another extension, this time in 'ministerial' style, designed by Sir Giles Gilbert Scott and Partners and dating from the early part of this century.

Masons Avenue

It is worth looking into the leafy area on the left, once the site of St Mary Aldermanbury and now a public garden. This church, designed by Wren and built between 1670 and 1686 at a cost less than half that of St Lawrence Jewry, was gutted in the last war with the result that only the tower, external walls and internal columns were left standing. By 1966 nothing remained except for the foundations, everything else having been shipped off to be rebuilt in Fulton, Missouri, as a memorial to Sir Winston Churchill. It is now an attractive verdant little space, an ideal lunchtime retreat.

Amongst the foliage along the path we come across a bust of Shakespeare perched on a pedestal. The sculptor was Charles Allen and it dates from 1893, the purpose being to commemorate Shakespeare's partners in the Globe Theatre venture, and his fellow actors, John Heminge and Henry Condell. It was they who gathered his collected works for publication in the first Folio edition of 1623. Notice also the granite drinking fountain on the corner with the pavement, about the only thing left that has stood its ground. It was originally built into the old churchyard wall in 1890.

St Alphage

On the corner with Basinghall Avenue we come to a rare survivor of the Blitz in the area, the Chartered Insurance Institute building of 1933, in a rather striking creamy white stone.

And now for the tricky bit, making the transition from here to the other side of London Wall. It is probably best to look at the map. We walk along the south side of Aldermanbury Square, glance quickly to our right to take in Brewers' Hall of 1960 by Sir Hubert Worthington, and continue to the end. Here we find a small dog-leg stairway. Proceed up the steps and enjoy your walk through Alban Gate.

The next place of interest is the remains of St Alphage. Who would have thought that medieval remains could have survived in such a spot? What we see is all that is left of the chapel for the Priory and Hospital of St Mary-within-Cripplegate, built in 1329. Sections of the chapel were modernised in 1777 but subsequently demolished in 1923.

We can descend to ground level and lose all sense of the proximity of busy London Wall. We can even climb the little spiral stair in the tower, but not too far!

The last antiquity in this area lies in St Alphage Gardens, which plays host to a well-preserved section of the City Wall. We arrive there by retracing our steps to the elevated walkway, continuing eastwards and dropping down into the garden. The northern side of the Wall is in fact more impressive than the face we see from the gardens.

And now to move on to Area M. Continue to the eastern end of the garden, up the steps, turn left and down the next flight. We cross London Wall and down the other side, spotting as we do so Girdlers' Hall, founded on the site in 1431, and, like Brewers' Hall, rebuilt in 1960. A small section of wall from the previous hall, rebuilt after the Great Fire, has been kept and forms part of the garden landscaping.

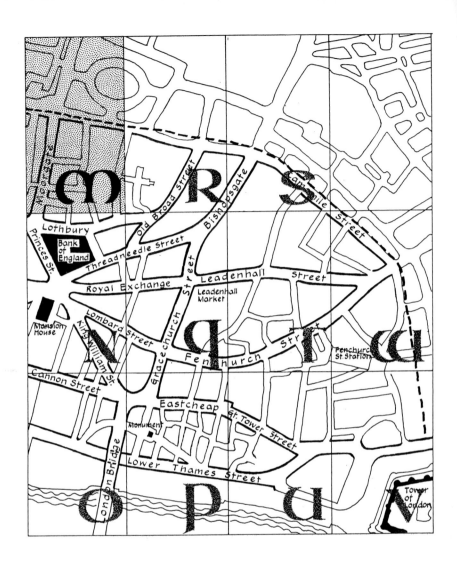

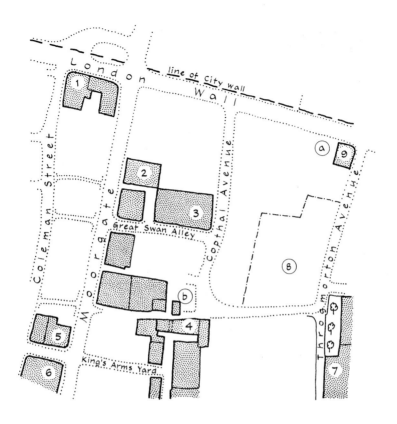

1 Armourers' and Braziers' Hall
2 Ocean Accident Company Building
3 Institute of Chartered Accountants
4 12 and 14 Tokenhouse Yard
5 15 Moorgate
6 7-11 Moorgate
7 Drapers' Hall
8 Site of Drapers' Gardens
9 2-2a Throgmorton Avenue

a The Talbot
b Butler's Head

baving walked along the south side of London Wall, we come to Armourers' and Braziers' Hall, sited on the corner with Coleman Street. The company have owned the site since 1428. Their pre-Fire building was demolished and a new one built in 1795. This in turn was replaced in 1840 by the one that we see today, designed by J.H.Good. Rather good fun was obviously had with the depiction at parapet level of the three painted figures in armour guarding the company's shield.

Coming back to Armourer's Hall, the collection of buildings between here and Moorgate were all built at approximately the same time that Moorgate itself was created in 1830. Two of the shops in Moorgate which form part of this block still retain the wonderfully delicate shopfronts, with unbelievably slender hardwood glazing bars and ornate applied carving along the head.

Back to Coleman Street, and we pass on the left a pleasing modern building with a flat facade of polished granite, incorporating an interesting stylised entrance opening onto the passageway called Coleman Street Buildings. Nothing much of interest remains until we come almost to the end of the street and numbers 7-11, Basildon House. This is quite a knock-out, with polished pink granite at ground and basement levels, grey granite columns between first and second storeys, and the rest modelled with great invention in Portland stone, the detail liberally applied like icing to a sumptious cake.

Cutting down King's Arms Yard we come to another striking building on the corner with Moorgate, this time numbers 13-15, a Grade II listed building of 1890-93 by Aston Webb and Ingress Bell, now occupied by the Arab Bank PLC. The corner treatment is a work of art, as indeed is the whole building, displaying throughout an impressive consistency of detail.

15 Moorgate

The remaining buildings in Moorgate are either post-war or inter-war. Two favourites are, on the right, Northgate House of 1937 by Sir Henry Tanner, with lions' heads separating each of the lead-clad bay windows, and, next, numbers 38–44. You will be quick to spot that this last building has a nautical theme about it. Large heads of Neptune form the keystones to the ground floor windows with, further up, carvings of sea-horses and prows of ships cutting through the waves. Included in all this is the nice little touch of a lighthouse in a niche on the corner. It is not surprising, therefore, that the building was originally the headquarters of the Ocean Accident Company, designed by Sir Aston Webb and Son and finished in 1928.

This brings us conveniently to Moorgate Place, a glazed-brick vaulted passage over which, at the far end, is the somewhat art nouveau 'Ocean Buildings' inscription, with ships in full sail on either side. This theme is taken up again over the entrance doorway of number 3 Moorgate Place, with a ship's prow bursting through both waves and pediment.

And now for a surprise, the Institute of Chartered Accountants' building by John Belcher, completed in 1893. What can one say about it? Certainly it is unexpectedly racy for such a headquarters, with plenty of young bare-breasted women over the heavily blocked columns. The entrance doorway, with arch and niche over, is a masterpiece of three-dimensional co-ordination with, on the corner, two figures straining to support the overhang, and a myriad of figures along the frieze. Just stand and stare!

Continuing southwards down Copthall Avenue to the end, we turn right into Telegraph Street. This is the introduction to a series of narrow passageways, at the centre of which is the Butler's Head public house.

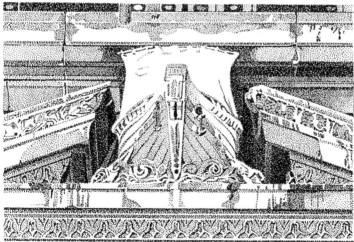

3 Moorgate Place

Opposite is a very narrow passageway running through numbers 12 and 14 Tokenhouse Yard, a very atmospheric corner tucked away behind Moorgate. Having walked through the passage, note the lovely reproduction Queen-Anne-style doorway to number 12, with its finely detailed broken-arched pediment supported by lions' heads and sporting a small mustachioed face leering down from above the door.

The next stage is to return, back up the passage and turn right towards Throgmorton Avenue. Before reaching there we pass, on our left, the site of Drapers' Gardens; real gardens, not the tower block office development of that name. The garden was purchased in the 1540s by the Drapers' Company, and formed a 'back yard' which extended northwards almost as far as London Wall. A public garden since the Great Fire, it steadily reduced in size until disappearing altogether in 1886 apart from the small, narrow, section we see at the end of the road, which originally formed the access to the Hall. You will note that it is now a private garden.

Turning right, we pass along the west side of Drapers' Hall and into Throgmorton Street, the start of Area N and the heart of the City, in general appearance somewhat reminiscent of the White Cliffs of Dover.

The Institute of Chartered Accountants

12 Tokenhouse Yard

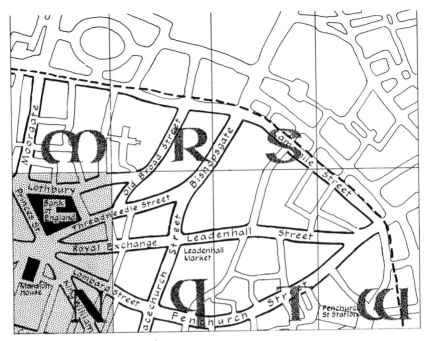

1   St Margaret Lothbury
2   7 Lothbury
3   National Westminster Bank
4   Drapers' Hall
5   Bank of England
6   Site of St Bartholomew by the Exchange
7   Site of St Christopher-le-Stocks
8   National Westminster Bank
9   Site of St Mildred Poultry
10 Site of St Mary Woolchurch
11 The Mansion House
12 St Stephen Walbrook
13 St Swithin's church garden
14 St Mary Abchurch
15 Site of St Nicholas
16 St Mary Woolnoth
17 Royal Insurance building
18 The Royal Exchange

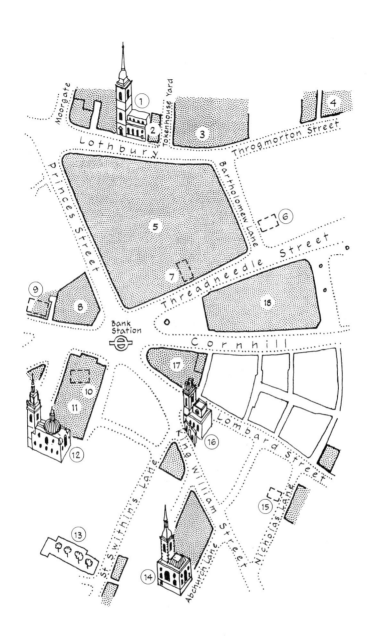

And so to Drapers' Hall. As mentioned in Area M, it was established on the site in the 1540's. The building we see today, with a long frontage embracing other occupants' entrances, dates from 1868-9 and was designed by Herbert Williams. He was seemingly an individualistic designer, one not influenced by the popular gothic, Tuscan or Venetian styles so exploited by his fellow contemporaries. The large and spectacular draped, appropriately, figures either side of the doorway were the creation of Sir T. Jackson and added ten years later.

Across the street is the Stock Exchange, a 1960s effort. Fortunately, the north side of Throgmorton Street has largely escaped the post-war blitz. Notice particularly the very attractive doorway of the Throgmorton Restaurant with 'J. Lyons & Co.' in wrought iron. We now pass back across the entrance to Throgmorton Avenue, complete with its large and impressive cast-iron gates bearing the motto 'Unto God be honour and Glory'. Next door is Warnford Court of 1884, in Portland stone with pink granite to the entrance. Unfortunately its neighbour, Slaters Restaurant, vanished in the 1980s to be replaced by the large faceless building which also occupies the site of Copthall Court. Next to this is the National Westminster Bank of 1923 by Mewes and Davis, a very large and stately Portland stone edifice.

The Throgmorton Restaurant

Crossing the end of Tokenhouse Yard, we come to a Victorian City building in the best extravagant design tradition of that era, number 7 Lothbury of 1866 by George Somers Clarke in a kind of neo-Venetian style, one of many influenced, one imagines, by Ruskin's book,'The Seven Lamps of Architecture' published in the early 1850s. The building is flanked by St Margaret's Close, a narrow passageway leading to the churchyard of St Margaret Lothbury. The church, by Wren, and built between 1686 and 1695 following the destruction of its predecessor in the Great Fire, is of an elegant simplicity. It also acts as a repository for some of the furnishings and fittings of City churches destroyed in the Georgian and Victorian eras. For example, St Christopher-le-Stocks: 1782: St Bartholomew by the Exchange: 1841, St Olave Old Jewry: 1888 and All Hallows the Great: 1894. If is a pity that the church, that once rose high above its surroundings, is now dwarfed by its neighbours, but we are fortunate that, with its wonderful internal fittings, it escaped damage in the War.

7 Lothbury

Between two Victorian bank buildings that complete the continuation to Moorgate we find Founders Court, a narrow passageway leading to what was the site of Founders' Hall. This was built in 1531 and destroyed in the Great Fire. Its replacement lasted until 1845 and the next one was let to the Electric Telegraph Company in 1854. The Founders then moved to a new hall, designed for them by George Aitchison, in St Swithins Lane which was completed in 1878.

Now on to the Bank of England, founded in 1694 by an enterprising Scot, William Patterson, and which operated from Grocers' Hall until 1734 when it moved to Threadneedle Street. From his appointment in October 1788 until his resignation in 1833, due to failing eyesight, Sir John Soane, a truly original and innovative architect, was commissioned to design and supervise the construction of a grand new building more commensurate with its dignity as a financial pillar of the Establishment. Unfortunately, the building created by Soane, in all its painstaking attention to space and detail met, as Lutyens might have described it, its 'Bakerloo' when, between 1921 and 1937, the Governors asked Sir Herbert Baker to 'scoop out' the inside and extend the single-storey building skywards. The external walls did not escape 'the treatment' either. One can only, even now after the lapse of time, look at the building and feel outrage that such an act of sheer vandalism could have been perpetuated. Photographs of the original interiors exist which have a strong power to excite the imagination, but which nevertheless cannot convey the three-dimensional quality and scale of the spaces that Soane was such a genius at creating.

Anyway, enough about this 'hobby horse'. Let us move on to Princes Street. The only point of interest here is the entrance to Grocers' Hall, which we touched upon in Area K. Walking quickly past the rather overbearing new-ish development on the right, we come to the National Provincial Bank building, now the National Westminster, of 1929 vintage by Sir Edwin Cooper and displaying none of the fun of his Port of London Authority building described in Area V. Having said this, the triumphal cluster of figures adorning the corner high above bring a touch of relief. A plaque on the wall notes that 'Near this spot the General Post Office stood in Post Office Yard 1653-66. Here were struck the first postmarks in the world. Philatelists take note!

Opposite, to the south, is the Mansion House, a fittingly monumental replacement for the more modest home of lord mayors until 1753, namely Williamson's Tavern. Strictly Palladian and built of Portland stone, it was designed by George Dance the Elder and constructed between 1739 and 1753. It would originally have looked far grander than it does today, surrounded as it would have been by buildings of a much smaller scale. Its immediate neighbour, the Scottish Provident building, was designed by Dunn and Watson and completed in 1915, and has a nice rhythmical sweep to the facade.

Dalou statue of mother and children

On the opposite corner is the Royal Insurance building of 1905 by Macvicar Anderson with its nicely rounded corner and eye-catching dome. It bears a plaque commemorating the site of the home of Thomas Guy (1644-1724), the founder of Guy's Hospital.

Crossing the road again we arrive at the forecourt of the Royal Exchange, and with it a chance to sit down and study the equestrian statue of Wellington, cast in 1844 by Sir Francis Chantrey, and to read the lengthy description of the origin of the material used in the casting. Across the road to our right lies the site of St Christopher-le-Stocks, sold in 1782 to prepare the ground for the new Bank of England. It was one of a few churches which in part survived the Great Fire, and was subsequently repaired by Wren, who also extended and embellished the tower in 1712, adding an obelisk at each corner with pineapples perched on the stone balustrading between.

Whilst looking in this direction we notice the strange sight of two pairs of naked men looking towards their rather demure female counterparts, mirrored around the central archway at the first floor level of the Bank. Quite what the significance of this is in relation to the function of the Bank of England I am not quite sure!

Behind us is the Royal Exchange, an early Victorian effort by Sir William Tite, built between 1841 and 1844 and opened by Queen Victoria. The first Exchange was opened by Queen Elizabeth I in 1570, the purpose of the building being that of providing an enclosed trading centre for City merchants. The building featured a large open quadrangle with arcade to the perimeter and shops above. It was a victim of the Great Fire, and was subsequently rebuilt to the designs of Edward Jarman in 1674. His building was similar to its predecessor in plan, and lasted until 1838 when it was destroyed by fire. Its replacement is the building that we see today, which has recently been extensively refurbished.

Continuing up Threadneedle Street, we come to Royal Exchange Buildings, a wide passageway at the rear of the Royal Exchange, presided over by a large bronze seated figure with hands clasped firmly to the sides. It is of George Peabody, the philanthropist, and was modelled by W. Story in 1869. Further east along Threadneedle Street is another sculpture, this time gracing a fountain, a delightful depiction of a mother and children by Jules Dalou, dated 1876.

Retracing our steps and cutting down Royal Exchange Buildings, we arrive in Cornhill and turn left into Change Alley and past the plaque commemorating the site of the King's Arms Tavern; it is worth a moment to read the inscription. Keeping on through the alleyways we reach Lombard Street where we turn left for a quick diversion to see the splendid doorway of numbers 24-28, situated just beyond Nicholas Lane. The building itself is by Gunton and Gunton, erected in 1910. However, to the doorway, which features a pair of voluptuous young women draping themselves on the arched pediment, guarded from below by a roaring lion's head.

Turning down Nicholas Lane we reach King William Street, and, there not being much of note, turn right and then left down Abchurch Lane to arrive at a small paved square that is graced by St Mary Abchurch. Designed by Wren, and built between 1681 and 1687, the church has a pleasingly modest exterior, of brickwork with stone dressings, which belies the wonderful quality of the interior. The dome, painted by William Snow and completed in 1708, covers the whole area of the church and thus results in one large uninterrupted area without nave or aisles. Quite an engineering feat on Wren's part. The church also contains the only authenticated work, outside of St Paul's, by the great wood-carver Grinling Gibbons, namely the lime-wood reredos installed in 1686. A vaulted crypt is all that remains of the pre-Fire church. As we leave, glance back at the graceful lead spire which sits so firmly on the tower.

St Mary Woolnoth

And so back to King William Street, laid out between 1829 and 1835 to connect London Bridge with the Bank, and to a church of unusual design and great inventiveness; St Mary Woolnoth. It was designed by Wren's amanuensis of many years, Nicholas Hawksmoor, who was noted for the originality of his work. The church, its lower reaches only recently freed from the clutches of the London Underground, was built between 1716 and 1727 on the site of its predecessor destroyed in the Great Fire. Unusually, the interior is in the form of a cube, and only the Corinthian columns pay homage to the classical tradition. It is a pity that it was the only church in the City to be designed by Hawksmoor, who's most famous ecclesiastical creations lie to the east in Spitalfields and Stepney.

Behind the church is the GPO building of 1951, interesting only in that it occupies the site of the General Post Office which operated here between 1678 and 1829 before moving to its vast new headquarters in St. Martins-le-Grand.

Across the road, and once more in Lombard Street, there is an interesting plaque on the wall of the Lloyds Bank building. It refers to the site of the home of Gregory de Rokesley, Chamberlain to Edward I and eight times lord mayor of London, between 1274 and 1281, and again in 1285. It

St Stephen Walbrook

is strange that he is not more famous than Dick Whittington, one can only assume that it is because he did not own a cat.

And now on to Mansion House Place for a visit to the church of St Stephen Walbrook. Built between 1672 and 1687 with spire added in 1717, it is generally regarded as Wren's finest City church. The body of the church takes the form of a Greek cross and its most memorable feature is the panelled dome, with lantern, above the crossing. Originally, the altar, with reredos, would have been sited at the east end, and the pews would have been arranged in the usual manner, that is, flanking the nave.

owever, as a result of recently completed restoration work, a new altar has been erected directly beneath the dome. A large carved block of stone, by Henry Moore, this new altar is more suggestive of human sacrifice rather than the more sober rituals associated with the Church of England, its location though is logical, sited as it is at the focal point of the church. Although the interior is rather stark and empty looking without pews, a feeling reinforced by the all-white decor, we can now appreciate to the full the grandeur, and simplicity, of the original concept. The abundant natural light plays on the curved forms and recesses, with the dome, the support arches above the Corinthian columns, and the arched fanlights all combining to stunning effect. So successful is the symetrical effect that is created, one is oblivious of the fact that the building is not square, a tribute once again to Wren's ingenuity in creating classical interiors within the confines of cramped and irregularly shaped medieval sites. The only slightly unhappy thing about the building is the relationship between the rather elaborate spire and the simplicity of the tower below, in fact it is difficult to discern any design element linking the two.

Before moving down to Cannon Street and into Area O, we should mention that Walbrook takes its name from one of the 'lost' rivers of London. Once the site of a dock in Roman times it is now confined and restricted beneath the streets on its way to meet the Thames.

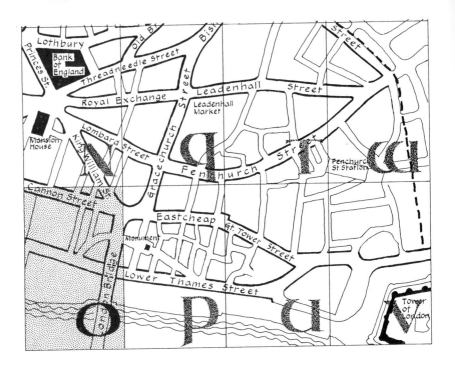

1　The London Stone and site of St Swithin
2　The Guardian Assurance building
3　St Clements
4　Site of St Michael Crooked Lane
5　Tower of St Martin Orgar
6　6 and 7a Laurence Pountney Lane
7　Site of St Laurence Pountney
8　1 and 2 Laurence Pountney Hill
9　Site of All Hallows the Great
10　Site of All Hallows the Less
11　Fishmongers' Hall

a　The Old Wine Shades
b　The Porter's Lodge
c　The City

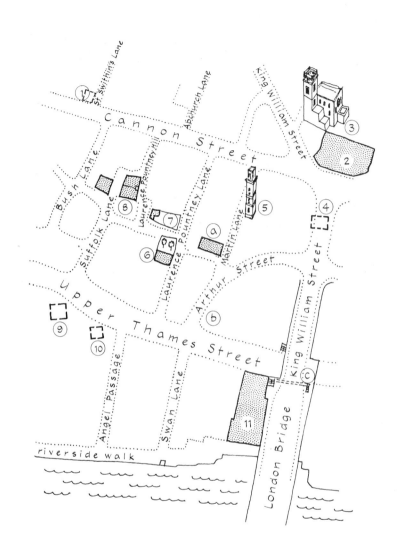

arriving at the southern end of Walbrook we turn left into Cannon Street, and a walk of a few yards brings us to the site of the church of St Swithin London Stone. This church, designed by Wren, and built between 1677 and 1687 to replace an older foundation destroyed in the Fire, was one of his more original designs. The body of the church took the form of a square which, via an octagonal intermediate stage, supported a dome, thus producing a clear internal space similar to that of St Mary Abchurch. The tower was interesting also, following as it did the same principle, with the transition from a square with cut corners to an octagon, and thence to a very tall slim lead spire. The London Stone, from which the church took its name, was originally a Roman milestone. Depicted in the earliest known map of the City of c 1550 as being sited opposite the church, it was incorporated by Wren into the south wall of his new church. Damaged by enemy action in the last war, and unfortunately not restored, the church was finally demolished in 1962. The Stone, which alone survived, is now embedded in the facade of the office building that currently occupies the site, one of the poorer examples of 1960s commercial design.

A few steps along St Swithin's Lane is the old church garden, its entrance flanked by a pair of rather nicely carved stone gate-posts topped with urns. A quiet, green oasis, typical of many such dotted throughout the City.

The London Stone

Laurence Pountney Vestry

O 94

The area south of Cannon Street was once a fascinating series of small lanes but is now stripped of historic interest apart from one or two that 'they' can't knock down (better not speak too soon). Cutting down Laurence Pountney Hill, referred to in Horwood's map of 1798 as Green Lettice Lane and by 1916 as Ducksfoot Lane, we discover, on our right, two treasures. These are numbers 1 and 2, with their lovely examples of early eighteenth century shell-hooded doorways. The railings have been replaced and the structure to the left is relatively modern, the previous building having returned hard against the entrance steps. As can be seen from the date on the left-hand hood, the buildings date from 1703 and both are Grade II listed.

At the junction with Gophir Lane stands the rather pretty Victorian vestry house of St Laurence Pountney, but where is the church you ask? The answer is as usual, that it was destroyed in the Great Fire. Opposite, in the corner, are numbers 6 and 7a, originally late seventeenth century, although at some stage something odd seems to have happened to the ground and first floor windows.

The Old Wine Shades

oving on eastwards through the Lane, we arrive at Martin Lane, with The Old Wine Shades on our right, a notable City pub housed in what is basically a late seventeenth century house, re-fronted in the eighteenth century. Originally it formed part of a terrace of similar houses, but now stands alone surrounded by modern neighbours. There is one exception, however, further up the lane on the left, namely that of the tower and rectory of what was once the church of St Martin Orgar. The buildings date from 1852 and were designed by John Davies. The style is Italianate and looks somewhat strange and out of place in its present surroundings. Mind you, even in its context a hundred years ago it would still have looked unusual.

We now head north, across Cannon Street, towards King William Street and left into Clements Lane for a visit to the church of St Clement East cheap. This was designed by Wren and built between 1683 and 1687 in a rather plain but nonetheless appealing style. The walls are of brickwork with cement render, which gives emphasis to the stonework tower with projecting stone quoins and a rather pleasing stone balustraded parapet. It is rather unusual to see a Wren tower as originally envisaged without the later addition of a spire. Also very welcome is the experience of leaving the busy main thoroughfare to walk up the quiet passageway against the north wall, leading to the churchyard. Here you can leave the modern City and step back in time.

Continuing along Clements Lane we pass, on the left, numbers 27 and 28, a yellow brick Victorian office building of 1864, with stone dressings and assorted heads forming keystones, which is a Grade II listed building. Next to this is Lombard Court, an atmospheric narrow passageway with a nicely proportioned round-headed stuccoed facade to the ground floor with brickwork over. This adjoins the Red Lion, a popular public house, its dark timber contrasting with the chequered arch and contrasting brick bands of the lively Victorian building which closes the court. Altogether a pleasant space.

We now retrace our steps to King William Street and then head south towards London Bridge. Approaching the bridge, we pass through the shade of the church of St Michael Crooked Lane, by Wren, which was demolished in 1831 to make way for the new access road. The second London Bridge, designed by Sir Charles Rennie and completed in 1831, lasted until 1968, when it was carefully dismantled and shipped to America for re-erection in the desert having been sold for £1 million. This transaction gave rise to the tenacious, but no doubt apocryphal, legend that the purchaser was under the impression that he was acquiring Tower Bridge.

On our right is Fishmongers' Hall designed by Henry Roberts and completed in 1834. It is in a monumentally classical style with giant Ionic columns designed to impress those crossing over into the City.

And now to Area P, approached by descending to Lower Thames Street.

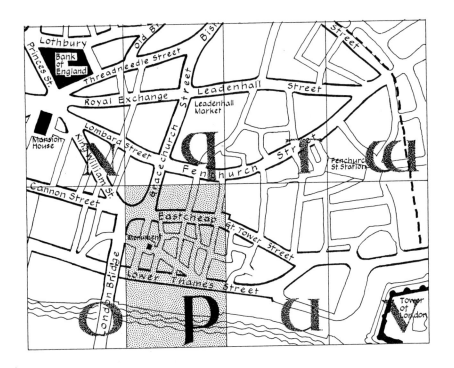

1 33-35 Eastcheap
2 St Margaret Pattens
3 St Mary at Hill
4 The Watermans' Company Hall
5 Site of the Coal Exchange
6 The Custom House
7 Billingsgate Market building
8 Site of St Botolph Billingsgate
9 St Magnus the Martyr
10 The Monument
11 Site of St Margaret on Fish Street Hill
12 Site of St George
13 Site of St Leonard Eastcheap

a The Ship
b Sir John Falstaff
c Balls Brothers Wine Bar
d The Walrus and Carpenter
e The Canterbury Arms

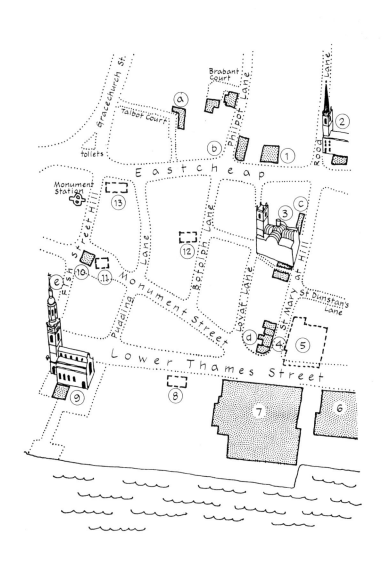

Gracechurch St.

Brabant
Court

Philpot Lane

Road Lane

Talbot Court

ⓐ

ⓑ

① ②

toilets

E a s t c h e a p

Monument
Station

⑬

Fish Street Hill

Botolph Lane

ⓒ

③

⑫

⑩ ⑪

Monument Street

Lovat Lane

St Mary at Hill

St Dunstan's
Lane

ⓔ

Pudding Lane

ⓓ

④ ⑤

L o w e r   T h a m e s   S t r e e t

⑨

⑧

⑦

⑥

baving arrived in Lower Thames Street, we can now visit the church of St Magnus the Martyr. The church has very close associations with Old London Bridge, the approach road having passed next to the western end by the tower. Thus it forms a landmark precisely locating the site of the original bridge.

The construction of Old London Bridge started in 1176, the architect being Peter, the curator of Colechurch in Cheapside (hence his official title of Peter de Colechurch). Unlike its three timber predecessors, the new bridge was built of stone and took thirty three years to build. It was 926ft. long, 20ft. wide and consisted of 20 arches, the space occupied by the starlings under the piers being 700ft. Thus, the river being 900ft. wide, one can deduce that the space left for the river to pass through was just 200ft. As can be imagined, this not only made things difficult for shipping, with frequent shocks to the piers, but the bridge also acted as a weir and at periods of extra high tides negotiating the arches must have been an experience akin to shooting the rapids. As with its predecessors, houses were a feature of the new bridge and, because it was one of the wonders of Europe, the buildings were of suitably fine quality, mostly owned by merchants. By the middle of the fourteenth century these numbered 198, so the walk across the bridge must have been rather like walking down a street, but with occasional views of the river. To the modern eye the pleasure of this walk would have been somewhat marred by the sight of the array of rotting heads that adorned the southern gateway, not exactly a cheery welcome to the metropolis!

St Magnus the Martyr

With the increase in commerce by the eighteenth century the impracticality of having a bridge with a carriageway of only 12ft. became such that an Act of Parliament was passed in 1754 for the removal of the houses remaining at the time. A temporary timber bridge was erected slightly to the East so that the work in removing the houses and increasing the width of the old bridge could proceed unhindered. As a result a carriageway of 31ft with footpaths of 7ft was created, and in 1759 Sir Robert Taylor and George Dance designed a large central arch to replace two smaller ones. And so the bridge remained, denuded and spruced-up, until its demise in 1831 in full view of the new structure by Sir Charles Rennie which had been started in 1824. Thus ended the long history of a structure that had survived for over six centuries. But now let us return to the present and the church of St Magnus the Martyr.

This church was designed by Wren and built between 1671 and 1687 to replace the previous one destroyed in the Great Fire (which, incidentally, also consumed almost half of the houses on the bridge). Parts of the old walls of the medieval church were incorporated in the new building. Its principle glory is the tower, one of the tallest in the City, with its octagonal belfry, lead cupola and spire, which were added in 1705. It was, no doubt, deliberately designed to impress the traveller approaching from the eminence of Fish Street Hill. This is still the best view today, even with the utilitarian backdrop of the rear of the otherwise impressive neo-Egyptian Adelaide House. In 1762 the aisles, which had previously extended to the western face of the tower, were shortened by one bay to expose the tower at ground level. This allowed a footpath to be created that ran through the tower and provided access to the bridge, which by now had been widened. These days we can walk round the side of the church to an open space with views of the river, passing on our way the church vestry, added in 1768.

Continuing eastwards down Lower Thames Street, whilst inhaling vast quantities of carbon monoxide, we pass the site of St Botolph Billingsgate, destroyed in the Great Fire and not rebuilt. At the same spot in those days we would probably have been ankle-deep in mire, inhaling smoke from a thousand chimneys and beset by a myriad of house flies and midges from the river. Add to this the stench of open sewerage and well, perhaps we are better off with the traffic.

The next building on the right is what used to be Billingsgate Fish Market, but which is now up for grabs for alternative use. The building dates from 1875 and was designed by Sir Horace Jones who also designed, if you recall, the Guildhall Free Library mentioned in area L. During its recent refurbishment there were fears that the melting of the hundred year old ice in the cellars beneath would cause the building to collapse, fears fortunately unfounded.

Slightly further along we arrive at the Custom House, a Grade I listed building with a rather long and ponderous facade in unrelenting yellow brick and of a size reflecting the importance of the Pool of London. It was designed by David Laing and built between 1813 and 1817.

Watermans' Hall

Crossing the street we arrive in St Mary at Hill. Once upon a time, in 1962 to be precise, a great act of vandalism was perpetrated at the eastern corner, namely the demolition of the Coal Exchange, a victim of the City's highway improvement schemes. Work on this building started in 1847, and the finished building was opened two years later by Prince Albert. It contained one of the most spectacular interiors in the City, with cast-iron galleries on three levels wrapping themselves around a glass-roofed rotunda, the whole sumptuously detailed as only the Victorians knew how. Or should I say as the designer J.B. Bunning knew how? Just over a century later, despite considerable public protest, demolition went ahead; the site remaining unoccupied for the next twenty years or so until the erection of the TSB building we see now.

The Monument

On the opposite corner is the Billingsgate Christian Mission Library and Reading Room, rather an imposing Victorian building, complete with little clock-tower, which until recently performed the function of a post office. Next to it is Watermans' Hall, built between 1778 and 1780, the design attributed to William Blackburn but with a delicacy more often associated with the Adam brothers. The facade is symmetrical, modest yet powerful and, most of all, eye-catching. Ionic pilasters flank an arched window, and although of narrow frontage, it stands out amongst its modest brick neighbours. Next door is a building of similar vintage, but in brickwork with arched windows, the one on the first floor with 'cobweb' glazing bars reflecting the style of its more illustrious neighbour.

The remaining buildings in the street are modern, apart from the church of St Mary at Hill further up on the left-hand side. This was designed by Wren and built between 1670 and 1676 for the modest sum of £3,980.

This delightful church presents two quite different faces to the visitor: the typical classical rear elevation we see here, and the later, simple brickwork tower with stone quoins and castellated parapet which can be viewed from Lovat Lane. The complex domed roof structure was completely destroyed by fire in 1988, but fortunately it has subsequently been lovingly restored.

The buildings either side of the church, numbers 6-8, are Grade II listed, numbers 6-7 being designed by Ernest George and Vaughan and built in 1873. A passageway through number 8, its entrance garnished with delightfully macabre skull and crossbones, leads into Lovat Lane. Originally Love Lane, this narrow sinuous street was largely rebuilt in the early 1980s. The style of the buildings is a pastiche of those that went before but they successfully retain the charm of a narrow City Lane winding down to the river. Although the cobbled surface has been kept, what is missing is the rattle of the costermongers' barrows echoing within its confines as they served the now non-existent shops. Cutting through Botolph Alley, again mostly modern, to Botolph Lane, which shares a similar treatment, we arrive opposite the site of the Wren church of St George. This was one of the first of the City churches to be rebuilt after the Fire, and was built between 1670 and 1677. It was sold for demolition and the redevelopment of the site in 1891. Unfortunately the southern view down Botolph Lane has now been closed off by the redevelopment of the Monument Street triangle, during which the continuation of the Lane was built over. In fact this whole area has now been given over to office buildings.

And now to Monument Street, Pudding Lane, Fish Street Hill and, of course, the Monument. This is an area which sustained minimal damage during the War but which has been almost completely redeveloped and rebuilt since. Included in this were the original Victorian buildings erected to line Monument Street when it was created between 1883 and 1893. The only ancient structure left, 'the untouchable', is the Monument itself. This was built to commemorate the spot nearby where the Great Fire broke out on Sunday the 2nd. September 1666. Its height of 202 ft. represents the distance from the base to the house in Pudding Lane where the Fire started. It was designed by both Wren and Robert Hooke and built between 1671 and 1677 on the site of St Margaret Fish Street Hill, destroyed in the Fire. The iron cage at the viewing gallery was added in 1842 for the security of those prepared to climb its 311 steps, and also to prevent a repetition of the six suicides that had occurred since its building. It appears that Hooke talked Wren out of his idea of finishing off the top with a statue of Charles II, the reigning monarch at the time. Instead he suggested the flaming gilt bronze urn, a more appropriate embellishment.

The original wording around the base attributed the cause of the Fire to Roman Catholics rather than to an accident in a baker's shop. The baker concerned, a Mr Farryner, when cross-examined subsequently, was able to prove that his shop had been locked up on the Saturday evening. Strangely enough, it was not until 1831 that this unjust inscription was removed. The view from the top is well worth the effort of the climb.

Αnd now to continue north up Fish Street Hill to Eastcheap, an ancient thoroughfare dating back to Roman times which was, in the Middle Ages, the site of a meat market. Crossing the street we come to Talbot Court which in spite of the backdrop remains a charming little dog-leg alley, the home of The Ship public house. Continuing eastwards we reach Philpot Lane where the only point of interest is Brabant Court on the left, approached through a passageway in number 6. This little corner has been spruced up in recent years with the result that its rather charming air of decrepitude has been lost.

The building on the east corner of Eastcheap and Philpot Lane, number 23, is but a foretaste to the amazingly flamboyant Victorian building further on, namely numbers 33-35 designed by R. Roumieu, and built in 1868. This is the most exotic example of its kind left in the City, and must have amused and astonished Londoners for generations.

Further eastwards we come to a memorable little cluster of early-Victorian shops abutting the church of St Margaret Pattens, designed by Wren and built between 1684 and 1689, mostly in Portland stone. The windows are well proportioned in what can be seen of the rather plain facade. The simple tower, with pinnacles at each corner, supports an outlandishly tall lead spire, which was finished in 1702.

And now on to an area crammed with interest, Area Q.

33-35 Eastcheap

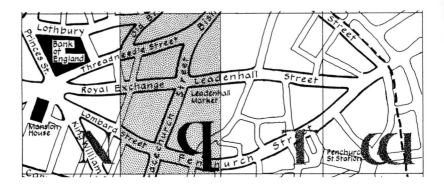

1 Site of the French Church
2 Facade of the National Provincial Bank
3 Site of St Martin Outwich
4 Merchant Taylors' Hall
5 Site of St Benet Fink
6 St Michael Cornhill
7 St Peter Cornhill
8 Union Discount Company building
9 St Edmund the King
10 Site of All Hallows Lombard Street
11 Site of St Benet Gracechurch Street
12 Site of St Dionis Backchurch
13 Leadenhall Market

a The Cock and Woolpack
b Simpson's
c The George and Vulture
d The Jamaica Wine House
e The New Moon
f The Swan Tavern
g The Lamb Tavern
h The Grapes
i The Red Lion
j The Ship

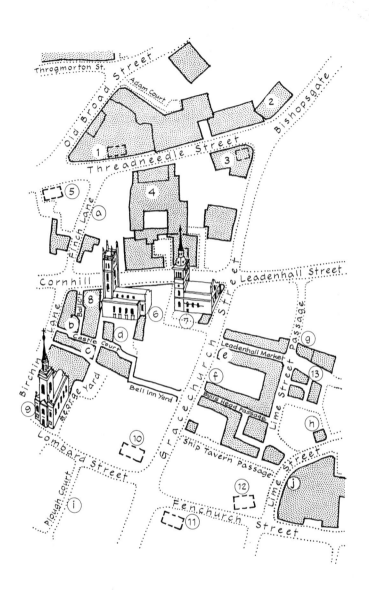

Throgmorton St.

Old Broad Street

Adam Court

Threadneedle Street

Bishopsgate

1

2

3

5

④

a

Finch Lane

Cornhill

Leadenhall Street

8

Ball

b

c

Birchin Lane

Castle Court

d

6

7

9

George Yard

Bell Inn Yard

Gracechurch Street

Leadenhall Market

e

f

Bulls Head Passage

Lime Street Passage

g

13

h

10

Ship Tavern Passage

Lombard Street

Plough Court

i

12

11

Fenchurch Street

Lime Street

j

Leadenhall Market

The northern end of Rood Lane brings us not only to Fenchurch Street but also to some rather fine buildings facing us on the other side of the road. These are number 153, in red brick, and its neighbour 151, in a very effective and simple Venetian style in Portland stone. For some reason the bulk of this building has been obscured by a screen of bronze-tinted glass panels. It was erected in 1976 and much admired by architects at the time.

Turning left and then right we come to Lime Street with, on the west side, the site of St Dionis Backchurch Street, rebuilt by Wren after the Great Fire. The church had simple round-headed windows to the aisles, a stone tower without spire, and a rather interesting interior featuring a vaulted ceiling to the nave and circular cut-outs to the clerestory windows. The church was sold for redevelopment and demolished in 1878.

Lime Street still has a Victorian air on the eastern side at least, where the bend in the road leads nicely into the small passages forming Leadenhall Market. The first of these is Ship Tavern Passage, although the pub that spans the end of the alley on Gracechurch Street is in fact the Swan Tavern. Next we come to Lime Street Passage, almost opposite which is Asia House, a highly individualistic building with the unusual feature of a broken pediment over the entrance door giving way to a vertical strip of inset bay windows above.

And so to the Market itself, where probably the best thing to do is to simply wander around the glass-roofed lanes comprising Bulls Head Passage and Whittington Avenue, admiring whilst you do so the richly detailed cast-iron work. The Market was designed by Sir Horace Jones and built in 1881. Sir Horace also designed Smithfield Market, slightly outside our area, and built fifteen years earlier. The elaborate embellishments look a little garish only because they have recently been picked out in primary colours, a nice contrast to the preponderant greys of the City outside.

Fortunately, unlike Billingsgate, this area survives as a working market. It was built on a site once occupied by a huge Roman basilica, or palace. In extent it stretched from Whittington Avenue westwards to St Michael's Alley in Cornhill, and was about 500ft. long and 150ft. wide. It comprised a vast aisled hall, which, together with a forum, or market place, to the south would have formed the principal administrative and commercial centre of London in Roman times. Mind you, the floor of all this occurs some 30ft. below where we stand today.

If we now walk down Leadenhall Street to Gracechurch Street we see not only the grand entrance to the Market, but also the two Victorian buildings, in red brick and stone, which flank it; these are in fact mirror images of each other and one of them houses the New Moon public house. Apart from the market itself, these two corners are all that remains of the predominantly Victorian character of an area which survived intact the ravages of war.

The best plan now is to proceed southwards down Gracechurch Street to the junction with Fenchurch Street. On the south-east corner stood, until its demolition in 1867 for road widening (does this have a familiar ring to it?), the Wren church of St Benet Gracechurch Street. Opposite is the richly detailed Portland stone Italianate building by H. and F. Francis of 1868 which houses Barclays Bank. The north west corner was once the site of the Wren church of All Hallows Lombard Street, built between 1686 and 1694, which survived until its sale in 1938 for redevelopment. A slight recompense must have been thought necessary when the decision was taken to re-site the tower alongside the A316 in Twickenham. This is obviously a popular site as it has seen its third redevelopment since the War, on each occasion rising to even greater heights.

We next cross over to Lombard Street, traditional home of the City's banking quarter since Lombard merchants came from northern Italy to establish themselves here in the twelfth century. The street is renowned for the many hanging signs which add to its special character.

At our present end of the street note the rather fine doorway to Barclays Bank at number 54. Further up on the right is the Wren church of St Edmund the King and Martyr, built between 1670 and 1679, a church which has witnessed many changes in its surroundings and, fortunately is one of the survivors. The roof required rebuilding following damage suffered during an air raid in 1917.

To the east side of the church is George Yard, gateway, so to speak, to the series of very narrow passages now quite unique in the City. Here you will find one of the narrowest facades in London which is a part of the George and Vulture public house, an eighteenth century hostelry in which Dickens housed Mr. Pickwick in his novel the Pickwick Papers. This is on the corner with the very narrow Bengal Court, which leads down to Birchin Lane. But by carrying straight on we come to Castle Court and The Jamaica Wine House next to the churchyard of St Michael Cornhill The Wine House is a rather striking red brick and red stone building of 1868, with inset bay windows and plenty of character. It is on the site of London's first coffee house, established in 1652 'at the sign of Pasqua Rosee's Head'. By the 1670s this had become The Jamaica Coffee House, frequented by those concerned with the Jamaica trade. Continuing on along Castle Court we arrive, on our right, at Ball Court and Simpson's Restaurant, a popular City hang out.

Ball Court leads, via a narrow passage, to Cornhill, on the corner of which is an exuberantly designed building of 1857 by H. and F. Francis housing the Union Discount Co. Next door to this is the Wren church of St Michael Cornhill. The original building was destroyed in the Great Fire, with only the tower remaining. This was patched up Wren when the body of the church was rebuilt between 1670 and 1677.

Ball Court

however, the tower was subsequently found to be unsafe and was rebuilt in the Gothic style by Wren's assistant Nicholas Hawksmoor between 1715 and 1721. The rather over-elaborate porch in high Victorian Gothic style was added by Sir George Gilbert Scott between 1857 and 1860. Perhaps it was thought necessary at the time to bring the entrance up to the same standard as its 'in vogue' neighbours.

A few yards up the road to the east we come to to another Wren church, that of St Peter Cornhill which is in total contrast to St Michael. It was built between 1677 and 1687 with an Italianate-style brick tower and lead steeple. The body of the church is finished in painted stucco. The whole is not easy to see from the pavement because of the shop built against the facade, so it is best to nip down St Peter's Alley to the church yard, a pleasant peaceful place isolated from the traffic, with its iron railings and stone flags beneath spreading plane trees. Alternatively, cross the road into Gracechurch Street where the strangely isolated east end can be seen, and from where the church and its clinging Victorian neighbours form a very pleasant composition.

Our tour continues by crossing over to the north side of Cornhill and walking west, The first turning we come to is White Lion Court where, by walking to the end and turning right, we get a view of the side of Merchant Taylors' Hall, with gable end and large chimneys all in white glazed brickwork. In fact, apart from their doorway in Threadneedle Street, and another small glimpse in Sun Court, this is all that can be seen of the Hall from the outside. However, parts of the original fourteenth century building do still survive within the Threadneedle Street facade designed by Beechcroft and built in 1844. The Company obtained its first Charter in 1327.

Cornhill itself is an ancient thoroughfare which, in the Middle Ages, was the main grain market in the City. It was also the site of a pillory and stocks, a rather uncomfortable and humiliating punishment.

One of their victims was no less a person than Daniel Defoe, who was forced to spend a day so confined in 1703 for publishing his broadsheet 'The Shortest Way with Dissenters'. Buildings of interest on the north side are numbers 66-67, designed by T. Chatfield Clarke and built in 1880, with plenty of carvings, the whole in Italianate style. Next to Sun Court is number 68, with well proportioned rectangular and round-headed windows, the theme of the latter picked up with the use of spherical lamps either side of the entrance. The building was designed by the Rolfe Judd group practice and built in 1985, it is one of the best modern buildings in the City. Also rather pleasant is number 73, a Grade II listed building of 1896 by G. Cuthbert, with carved figures supporting the overhanging cornice.

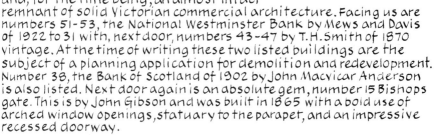

Glancing back across the road we see a building in a rather unusual style for the City and one of our favourites. This is number 55, in red terracotta with an angled turret and large gable sporting a crouching gremlin at its apex. The building was designed by Ernest Runtz and built in 1893. One wonders how many habitues of Cornhill are aware of this grinning demon perched precariously above their heads!

Moving further west we come to Finch Lane and number 2, with plenty of interest in the stonework designs to the ground floor which include bearded heads staring down at passers-by. The lion adorning the shell motif also looks as though it means business.

On reaching the end of Finch Lane we arrive at the continuation of Threadneedle Street and, for the time being, an almost intact remnant of solid Victorian commercial architecture. Facing us are numbers 51-53, the National Westminster Bank by Mews and Davis of 1922 to 31 with, next door, numbers 43-47 by T.H.Smith of 1870 vintage. At the time of writing these two listed buildings are the subject of a planning application for demolition and redevelopment. Number 38, the Bank of Scotland of 1902 by John Macvicar Anderson is also listed. Next door again is an absolute gem, number 15 Bishopsgate. This is by John Gibson and was built in 1865 with a bold use of arched window openings, statuary to the parapet, and an impressive recessed doorway.

The next stage is to retrace our steps down Threadneedle Street and then turn right into Old Broad Street. On our left are numbers 2-3 with a particularly unusual entrance door incorporating an art nouveau clock supported by wonderfully sculpted fishes draped with seaweed. This theme is taken up again with pairs of fishes lying dormant with tails coiled, mirrored either side of a shell resting on the window guard-rail. Numbers 10-11 are an inter-war building of 1925 by Gunton and Gunton; whilst 13-17 is considerably older, 1861 to be exact, by Clifton, in a regimented, strictly proportioned style which has a Grade II listing.

The next building of note is the City of London Club by Philip Hardwick (who, if you recall, also designed Goldsmiths' Hall) built in 1833-4 in a restrained classical style. Adjacent is Adams Court, an interesting little passage with wrought iron gates leading to an Italianate courtyard. Walking back down the Court affords a nicely framed view of number 26 Throgmorton Street designed in opulently-detailed Venetian style, with, next door, number 123 Bishopsgate, a rather more subdued design that incorporates the entrance to Austin Friars and the start of Area R.

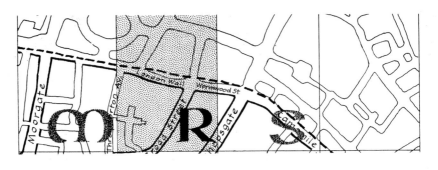

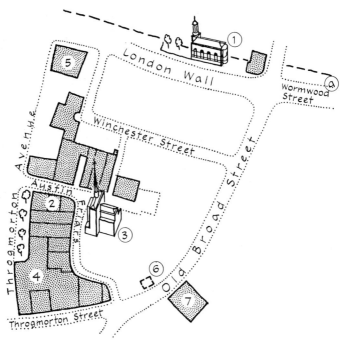

1   All Hallows by the Wall
2   23 Austin Friars
3   The Dutch Church
4   Drapers' Hall
5   Carpenters' Hall
6   Site of St Peter-le-Poor
7   The City Club   a   The Kings Arms

So, off to Austin Friars and the start of a delightful walk around narrow streets in which all of the buildings are noteworthy. Passing under the archway and turning the bend we have, on our left, number 31, of 1870, with its entrance in Throgmorton Street. Number 28 is very pleasant indeed, with large arched windows to the ground floor and red brick with cream-coloured stone window surrounds including decorated spandrel panels; it was designed by Sir Charles Reilly and built in 1894. Number 25 is very recent, 1991 in fact, and blends very well with its older neighbours.

This whole area is closely associated with the Dutch Church, which stands on the site previously occupied by what was originally the conventual priory of the Austin Friars, founded in 1253 by Humphrey Bohun. The priory was rebuilt in stone in 1354, was 'dissolved' in 1538, and twelve years later was granted to Protestant refugees from the Netherlands. This unique fourteenth century building, the subject of restoration works in the 1860s, was destroyed by enemy action in 1940. The present church was built in 1950, a good example of the ecclesiastical design of that period.

Turning left we find, on the left, number 23, a daring design, as one would expect from Aston Webb and Ingress Bell, who were responsible for that other master piece, number 15 Moorgate, described in Area M. Anyway, back to this building, with its very large round-headed windows laid out symmetrically, and what seems to be a minimum amount of Portland stone supporting the whole. The building dates from 1888. The other buildings in the street also date from the 1880s, and although nicely designed, seem rather tame in comparison with their neighbour.

23, Austin Friars

On the north side, we come to a terrace of three, of which number 14 is of red brick and stone and dated 1882. Number 13, in Portland stone, is rather a contrast, but we return to the red brick theme again with number 12, by E. Gruning, built in 1883 and set off nicely by the Queen Anne-style canopy to the doorway. This is an area where all of the buildings and the road pattern combine to produce a delightful little corner.

We can now turn left into Austin Friars Passage, which runs alongside number 12. Towards the end, on the left, you will notice a small length of brick wall, only 12 ft. long and 12 ft. high, which is obviously much older than anything surrounding it. If we pass through the door opening, with a small arched aperture above, we can see a stone tablet let into the wall with the initials P P and the date 1715. Looking at Rocque's map of 1745, it would appear to have formed part of the garden wall of a property flanking what was then called Bell Alley.

At the end of Austin Friars Passage we turn left into Winchester Street and approach, on the corner, a building that stands out from its neighbours only in that it boasts the unusual feature of an enlarged alcove lined with Ionic pilasters set back from the ground floor, with a large triangular pediment over the entrance doorway.

At the end of the street and to the left, in London Wall, we come to Carpenters' Hall, standing out conspicuously as a civic rather than commercial building. It was designed by W. F. Pocock and built in 1876, but suffered a direct hit in the last war which destroyed the interior. Whinney, Son and Austen Hall subsequently redesigned the Hall, work on which was completed in 1956. The company's first hall, built in 1429 on a site nearby, survived the Great Fire but was demolished in the early 1870s to make way for the creation of Throgmorton Avenue and the closure and subsequent development of Drapers' Gardens for commercial purposes.

Further east along London Wall we come to the church of All Hallows London Wall, known at the time of the Great Fire as All Hallows-in-the-Wall. The small churchyard garden is interesting in that the boundary wall is in fact a remnant of the original City wall. The lower stone courses are medieval, with later brickwork above. As to the church, it was built between 1765 and 1767 to the design of George Dance the Younger, and replaced the medieval one on the same site that had survived the Great Fire. Externally the church is eye-catching in its simplicity and was uncompromisingly 'new' in its time. It was much admired by the 15 year-old John Soane, who entered Dance's office a year after it was completed, and who considered it a novel break from the strict classical values held at the time.

And now to continue on eastwards along London Wall and the start of Area S.

All Hallows London Wall

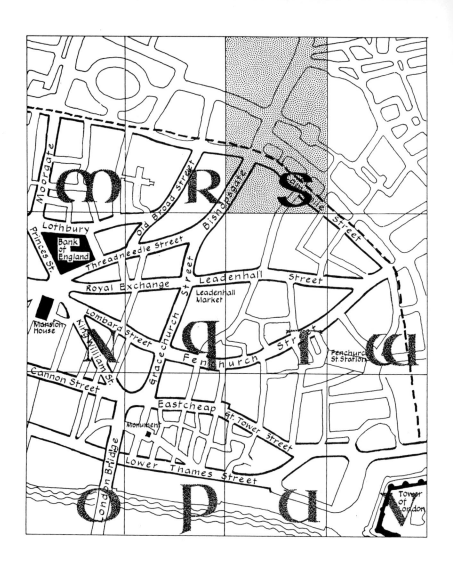

Moorgate
Lothbury
Princes St.
Bank of England
Threadneedle Street
Old Broad Street
Bishopsgate
Street
Royal Exchange
Leadenhall
Street
Leadenhall
Market
Mansion
House
Lombard Street
Gracechurch
Street
Fenchurch
Street
King William St.
Fenchurch
St. Station
Cannon Street
Eastcheap
Gt. Tower Street
Monument
London Bridge
Lower Thames Street
Tower
of
London

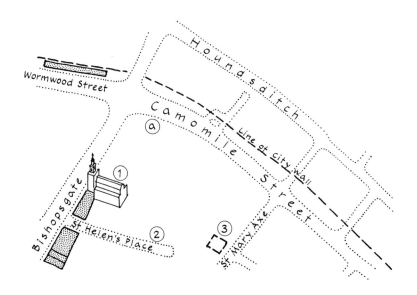

1 St Ethelburga the Virgin
2 The Leathersellers Company
3 Site of St Mary Axe

a The Mail Coach

rea S presents a bit of a problem in that very little of the older City remains, and most of what was left has been destroyed or seriously damaged in the terrorist bomb outrage of April 1993.

Carrying on from where we left off in Area R, we arrive in Wormwood Street, the continuation of London Wall. In the early 1970s this was a narrow street, less than half the width of London Wall, and lined with predominantly Victorian buildings. Then the road improvement scheme came along and those on the right were cleared away. A few still survived on the left higher up, including Wormwood Chambers in red brick with stone bands. Alas, all of these buildings were damaged by the bomb and their long term future is doubtful. The road-widening mania continued south eastwards along Camomile Street and Bevis Marks, so nothing of note remains there now.

If we turn right into Bishopsgate (the gate in the City wall was demolished in 1761, only thirty years after the original medieval gate had been rebuilt) we see across the road all that is left of historical interest in the whole area. Incidentally, it is worth mentioning that all except one of the pre-war buildings that lined Bishopsgate survived enemy action, which makes one realise the scale of the recent redevelopment of the area.

But to come back to the buildings in question. Firstly the church of St Ethelburga the Virgin, now sadly merely a derelict site, the complete facade and majority of the interior having suffered the full force of the explosion in 1993. The church was rebuilt between 1390 and 1400, and was one of only six left in the City that had survived the Great Fire. Apart from some cosmetic alterations made down the centuries, it had survived the ravages of time, fire, and war, and remained a cherished relic of the medieval City. The present position is not hopeful, but it is to be hoped that at some future date, when money is no longer considered to be the only criterion, St Ethelburga will rise again resuming her modest but charming role as a reminder of times past and a symbol of the enduring City.

Adjoining the site is the massive Banque Indosuez, which started life in 1928 as Hudson's Bay House, designed by Mewes and Davis. It incorporates a large archway entrance to the private thoroughfare of St Helen's Place, all of the buildings in which date from the 1920s, including Leathersellers' Hall towards the end. The attractively designed cast-iron gates bear the company's coat of arms

At the end of the Banque Indosuez we have a smattering of smaller-scale buildings, the best of which is number 48 with its very elaborate use of stonework that makes the most of a narrow 1890s frontage.

With this we come to the end of Area S, but a little more of interest should be found in Area T.

St Ethelburga the Virgin

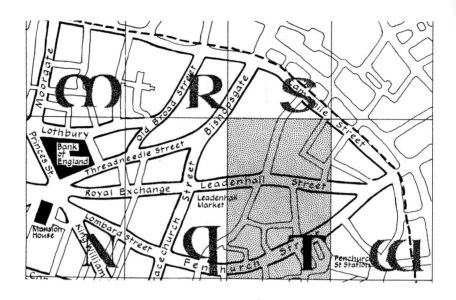

1   St Helen Bishopsgate
2   Site of the Baltic Exchange
3   1-4 and 32 Bury Street
4   St Andrew Undershaft
5   Remains of original Lloyds building
6   Bolton House, Cullum Street
7   Site of St Gabriel Fenchurch
8   Tower of All Hallows Staining
9   Site of Blanch Apleton church
10 Fenchurch Street Station

a   The Underwriter
b   The Ship and Turtle
c   The Wine Lodge
d   The Elephant
e   The Ship and Compass
f   The East India Arms
g   The City of London Yeoman

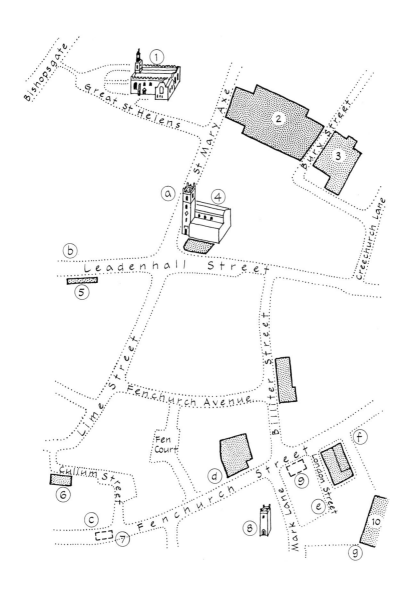

Continuing along Bishopsgate we turn left and enter Great St Helens. The roadway, churchyard and church are still as shown on John Leake's 'Exact Surveigh' of 1667, which was commissioned by the City authorities to indicate the extent of the damage caused by the Great Fire a year earlier. Whilst the church has remained virtually unchanged since that time, everything around it is in a constant state of flux.

The church of St Helen started life as the Benedictine nunnery of St Helen, and remained so until its dissolution in 1538. As originally planned, the north aisle formed the Nuns Quire (choir), the southern aisle serving as the parish church. The nuns' living quarters were situated to the north of the church. The bell tower dates from the seventeenth century, as do the heavily carved oak doors with their stone surround and pediment dated 1633. No doubt the style of these features owes something to the influence of Peter Mills, Master bricklayer to the City, who lived between 1600 and 1670, and who would have been fully aware of the current renaissance revival led by Inigo Jones. In fact Jones had been appointed Kings Surveyor in 1615, and had commenced an extensive programme of repairs to St Paul's Cathedral in 1628. The windows, some original and some Victorian additions, were victims of the IRA bomb on election day 1992.

St Helen

If we carry on past the church, we arrive in St Mary Axe almost opposite the site of the Baltic Exchange, a Grade II listed building designed by T.H.Smith and Wimble and built between 1900 and 1903. Unfortunately this fine building has been recently demolished due to damage suffered as a result of the 1992 bomb.

St Mary Axe derives its name from the church which existed on the other side of the street slightly further north. It is shown on the earliest known map of the City, drawn in 1550, but does not appear on Leake's map of just over a century later. The reason for this, as Stow records, is that the church was converted to a warehouse in 1565, when the parish was united with that of St Andrew Undershaft, on the south-east corner with Leadenhall Street. This church was, at the time of the map, fairly new, the body having been built between 1520 and 1532.

T he tower was a century or so older, but was largely rebuilt in 1830. The church, like St Helen, suffered damage in the IRA bomb blast of April 1992. One hopes that the alabaster monument of Stow, who was buried in the church, has not been badly affected.

There remains a pleasantly 'in scale' building next to St Andrew: numbers 113-116, a late Victorian development with oriel windows under a small tower that sets off the corner very successfully.

Looking west down Leadenhall Street it is hard not to notice the new Lloyds Building by Richard Rogers, the only stainless steel building in the City, whose nautical associations are hinted at in its 'oil rig' form of treatment. It was erected on the site of their previous Grade II listed headquarters, the only part of this building now surviving being the facade of the main entrance, which was designed by Sir Edwin Cooper and completed in 1925.

Lloyds has always traditionally been associated with marine insurance, a business originally conducted in coffee houses, the first being in Tower Street in the 1680s. From there they moved to Abchurch Lane and thence, in 1769, to Lloyds Coffee House in Pope's Head Alley (between Cornhill and Lombard Street). A short time later they moved to offices in the Royal Exchange, and finally finished up in their own headquarters building in Leadenhall Street in 1925.

If we continue eastwards along Leadenhall Street we arrive at Bury Street, which is well worth a visit in order to see one of the most unusual office designs in the City, numbers 1-4 and 32, designed by Hendrik Berlge, a leading Dutch architect and built in 1914. The first stage of the building consists of a polished black granite plinth, with a stylised representation of a ship's prow on the corner. The upper floors consist of very light grey/green glazed tiles on closely spaced slender columns, such that, when viewed from an angle, the building does not appear to have any windows at all. Altogether it is a most unusual and original design, very advanced for its date, and a precursor of the future developments in the design of office buildings. It is well worthy of its Grade II listed building status.

St Andrew Undershaft

But now to return to Leadenhall Street, and thence
left into Billiter Street and
the only building left of any note,
that of numbers 19-21, dated 1865.
It is built in white stone, relieved
at the ends by contrasting red
stone quoins and polished pink
granite divisions, the windows
decorated with cherubs and, once
more, the prow of a ship over the
doorway.

This nautical theme is taken up
again in more dramatic fashion
down the road at number 60 Fenchurch Street, where large sea
figures, mermen judging by their
tails, strain to support the overhanging upper floors on the corner
of the building. Around the corner
is Fenchurch Street Station with
its striking yellow brick frontage,
a part of the original station, dating from 1853 and designed by
George Berkeley. It was the first
railway terminus to connect the
City with Blackwall. The line when
first opened in 1841, finished at what
was then called Blackwall Station in
the Minories nearby, and was later
extended to Fenchurch Street.

32, Bury Street

If we now glance westwards from the station, we are perhaps surprised to
see a small, solitary tower, all that remains of another medieval church,
All Hallows Staining. The tower dates from the fifteenth century and has
recently been restored.

Further westwards along Fenchurch Street we come to Fen Court, a paved
open space with a few tombstones dotted around that now serve as lunch
tables for office workers. This was once the site of the churchyard of St
Gabriel which was destroyed in the Great Fire and not rebuilt, although
the tombstones that we see don't look quite that old.

Slightly further along on the left we have Plantation House, a very large building whose main frontage, with its two splendid doorways, is in Mincing
Lane. It was designed by A.W. Moore and completed in 1937, although it
does in fact look older. The interior has recently been comprehensively
refurbished, a welcome decision and far preferable to the demolition
for which planning permission had been granted.

All Hallows Staining

Further along Fenchurch Street, on the right, let's make a small detour into Cullum Street to see an absolute beauty. This is Bolton House, of 1907 vintage and a riot of colour. With its green and white tiling to the second floor, brown glazed bricks and green window surrounds below, pale blue tiled panels with 'Bolton House' as the motif, and a wonderfully scrolled green frieze, it is definitely a most worthy candidate for listed building status.

Opposite the entrance to Cullum Street, and right in the middle of Fenchurch Street, stood Fen Church, destroyed in the Great Fire.

Now back to Mincing Lane which is on our route to Area U.

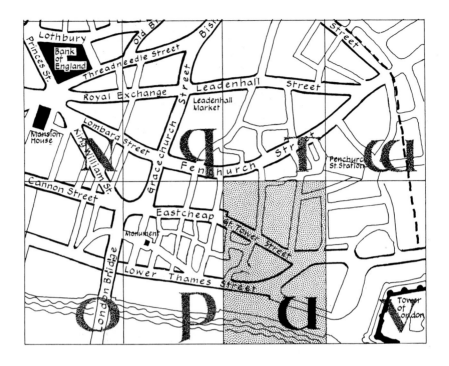

1 St Olave Hart Street
2 59-60 Mark Lane
3 Corn Exchange Chambers
4 All Hallows Barking
5 National Westminster Bank and Christ's Hospital buildings
6 The Custom House
7 Remains of St Dunstan in the East
8 Entrance to Plantation House

a The Ship

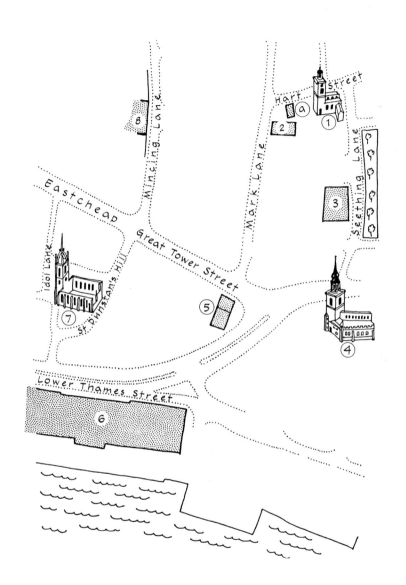

Hart Street

Mark Lane

Wincing Lane

Seething Lane

Eastcheap

Idol Lane

Great Tower Street

St. Dunstan's Hill

Lower Thames Street

So, having admired the gilt embellished stonework surrounds to the entrances of Plantation House, we carry on down Mincing Lane, concious of the polished pink granite modern 'gothic' Minster Court looming on our left. Lots of money has been spent on both schemes, past and present.

Crossing Great Tower Street, we then carry on down St Dunstan's Hill to what remains of St Dunstan in the East, victim of a swathe of bombing, north to south, that blitzed the City from Camomile Street to the river. As can be seen, the tower and part of the body of the church survived, but regrettably have not been restored. The original church was partially destroyed in the Great Fire, and Wren was employed to rebuild the tower, which was completed in 1698 in a highly original and imaginative gothic style. The idea of using flying buttresses bordered by four pinnacles to support a very slender and graceful spire was quite masterly, in fact it is unique in City churches. The shape of the space created by the buttresses is carried down through the window heads to the arched doorway. Wren obviously enjoyed himself devising this composition! What little remains of the body of the church dates from the rebuilding of 1817 and 1818 and forms the enclosure of a delightful garden, probably the best in the City. The slope down to the river is at its steepest here which adds considerably to the feeling of being in a terraced garden.

St Dunstan in the East

Moving down to that 'Hell of the South', Lower Thames Street, we arrive opposite the somewhat uninspiring facade of the Custom House, mentioned in Area P.

If we can bear to walk eastwards we will come to the corner with Great Tower Street and two very finely detailed brickwork facades in late seventeenth century style. The buildings stand cheek by jowl, the first being Christ's Hospital offices with the National Westminster Bank offices adjacent, both designed by Sir Reginald Blomfield and built in 1914. These are well worthy of closer inspection despite the immediate surroundings which are dominated by the unspeakably grim wasteland of the Bowring development. With its bleak, joyless, appearance blighting the approaches to the Tower, it is surely one of the worst of the 1960's office developments.

Further east we catch sight of a church with many different faces, a fascinating amalgam of brickwork and stone both ancient and modern. This is All Hallows Barking, a survivor of the Great Fire but not of the bombing in the last war, which destroyed part of the nave. Starting out as an abbey on land endowed by Eorconweald, Bishop of London, in 675, it was rebuilt in Saxon times, then extensively modified and extended in the thirteenth, fourteenth and fifteenth centuries. In 1658-59 the tower was completely rebuilt following damage, which affected the whole of the west elevation, caused by an enormous explosion involving over two dozen barrels of gunpowder. Needless to say not only the church was affected. The tower is interesting in that it is the only example of church building in the City of the Cromwellian era. It is odd that the tower was built at such a jaunty angle with the rest, unless of course it followed the original imprint. Odder still, though, is that something seems to have happened to it since the war. The top of the tower has acquired a strongly modelled cornice and the previous 'spire', if one can call it that (a small cupola with little louvred openings below), has been transformed into an impressive full-blown 'Wren-type' baroque number.

Crossing over Byward Street, a thoroughfare created at the turn of the century, we arrive in Seething Lane, leafy on the right and with what looks like a pre-war building on the left. Surprisingly, though, it dates from 1859. It has stone arched windows to the ground floor and the red brickwork above is pierced by arched windows in rectangular stone surrounds. The leafy area opposite is Seething Lane Gardens, a pleasant, narrow strip of vegetation, welcome in the City and built, or should one say fostered, on a site once occupied by the Navy Office, which disappeared in 1788. Adjacent to this was the house of the area's greatest personality, indeed one of England's, namely the diarist Samuel Pepys, who lived there between 1660 and 1673.

he worked in the Navy Office, initially holding the post of Clerk to the Privy Seal and later Secretary to the Admiralty. He also wrote his diaries in this house, starting in January 1660 and ending in May 1669, although it was not until 1825 that the first half of them were published, following the laborious process of deciphering Pepys' personal form of coded shorthand. He retired from the Navy Office in 1688, was imprisoned twice, in 1680 and 1690, became a Justice of the Peace in the early 1660s and an MP in 1673. He was one of the founding presidents of the Royal Society and, in 1690, published his 'Memoirs of the Royal Navy'. He died on the 26th May 1703 and is buried in the church of St Olave, Hart Street, which he had attended regularly and which is our next stop.

You will find the church at the end of Seething Lane on the left-hand side. The entrance to the churchyard is through a large stone work gateway, dating from 1658, with pediment embellished with human skulls and flanked by a skull on each side. The church is a survivor of the Great Fire, but the interior and the fifteenth century roof were destroyed in the last war. However, ancient parts remain, including a section of the west wall of the nave with crypt below which date from the thirteenth century. The main parts of the church date from the fifteenth century, it was later restored in 1632 - 33, with the vestry being added in 1661. It was refaced in 1693, and the top of the tower was rebuilt in brick between 1731 and 1732 by John Widdows. Internally the church has a strong 'pre-Fire' feel, which says a lot for the skill of the restorers. This atmosphere is enhanced by the wonderful sixteenth century monuments, some coloured, and all fascinating works of art.

If we now turn into Hart Street, we come across a building on the left of an altogether lighter character. This is the Ship public house, a delightful Victorian building, its narrow stonework facade adorned with vines and bunches of grapes all picked out in brilliant colour.

The only other building of note in this area is round the corner in Mark Lane, this is numbers 59 - 60, an office development of circa 1870 built in stone in the ever popular Venetian style.

And now on to Area V, which is best approached by retracing our steps and returning down Seething Lane, thence turning left into Muscovy Street.

St Olave Hart Street

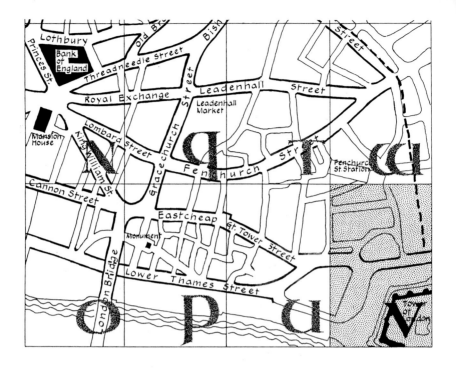

1 Port of London Authority building
2 Trinity House
3 Trinity Square Gardens
4 Second World War Mercantile memorial
5 First World War Mercantile memorial
6 Site of the scaffold, Tower Hill
7 Wakefield Gardens
8 Exposed portions of the City wall
9 The Tower of London

a The Bulla
b Ye Olde English Clubbe

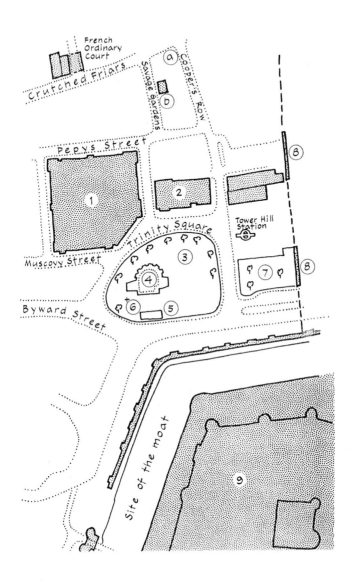

French
Ordinary
Court

Crutched Friars

Coopers Row

Savage Gardens

ⓐ

ⓑ

Pepys Street

1

2

8

8

Trinity Square

3

4

5

6

Muscovy Street

Byward Street

Tower Hill
Station

7

8

Site of the moat

9

uscovy Street brings us to what was, until a couple of decades ago, the Port of London Authority Building. The vast head-quarters reflected the scale of activity in the docks and Pool of London of decades ago, which are now all but dead. The building itself dates from 1912-22 and was designed by Sir Edwin Cooper, to reflect the time when Britain 'ruled the waves' in both naval and mercantile capacities. At least the building still survives! Note the statue of a bare breasted woman lounging back against the east wall of the building, her left hand firmly grasping the wheel of an imaginary ship, whilst her left foot both props and restrains a buoy: truly the embodiment of Britannia. Her male counterpart can be found round the corner. Both are by A.H. Hodge, who also provided the giant figures that adorn the triumphal centre-piece higher up. Altogether quite a tour de force.

Next door we have Trinity House, very modest by comparison, and restored after damage caused in the last war. The building was designed by Samuel Wyatt and built between 1792 and 1794. It has a well proport-ioned stonework facade with Ionic capitals to the pilasters, a design feature typical of this period.

Crossing over the road we arrive in Trinity Square Gardens, once the site of the scaffold, but now housing memorials to merchant marine casualties in the the First World War and also to merchant navy and fishing fleet casualties in the Second World War. The First World War memorial, in Portland stone clad with inscribed bronze tablets, was designed by Sir Edwin Lutyens. The Second World War memorial is less formal, being a sunken garden, the retaining walls of which are lined with tablets listing the names of those killed from each county. The design of the gardens has been very sensitively handled: they also serve as a public open space.

And now to the Tower of London, tourist attraction par excellence, which, strictly speaking, should not be included in this work as it officially lies outside the City walls, in fact in the London Borough of Tower Hamlets. Anyway, just a quick word about it. The heart of the Tower and the outer defences were built in the eleventh century between 1078 and 1098, the centrepiece, and the oldest part, being the White Tower so named by rea-son of the white Caen stone from which it was built. The bulk of the second line of defences, which incorporate the Wakefield Tower, were built in the reign of Henry III, 1216-72, and the final, outer, walls including the Byward and Middle Tower's either side of the moat, were completed in the reign of his son Edward I. In all their long years these impressive fortifications were never subjected to the test of battle.

For the full experience you'll have to run the gauntlet of the crowds and fight your way in, having first acquired your copy of the Official Guide. It was in hosting visitors that the Tower came into its own over the cent-uries, and many were the famous guests who passed through its gates, many never to return. Before passing on we must mention the Crown Jewels, made in 1661 for Charles II by Sir Robert Vyner, supplemented by many later artifacts, including the Imperial Crown of India of 1911.

The original Crown Jewels were broken up and dispersed following the execution of Charles I, presumably on the assumption that they would not be needed again. Their replacements were almost disposed of in their turn by Colonel Blood, who, in a daring attempt in 1671, stole them and actually got out of the Tower before being caught. Surprisingly he was pardoned by King Charles II, for reasons unknown.

The next stop is Wakefield Gardens, named after Viscount Wakefield of Hythe, who lived at number 41 Trinity Square and who, with his wife, led the Tower Hill restoration earlier this century. Wakefield Gardens is a small open area, part of which is taken up by a large bronze sundial with pictorial themes of London around its perimeter. At the eastern end there is a large section of Roman wall. Another, more impressive length, will be found by continuing up Trinity Square and turning right past numbers 42-43. A small guide by the wall mentions that the lower courses up to the last red brick band is of Roman origin whilst that above is medieval.

having inspected the wall from both sides, we now head north and then turn left into Pepys Street and right into Savage Gardens, passing on our right Ye Olde English Clubbe public house, still retaining the air of a warehouse with loading derricks serving the upper level doorways.

And so to Crutched Friars, the interest being supplied by number 42 across the road. This is an early eighteenth century brick house, very nicely proportioned and detailed with stuccoed courses to the ground floor, the theme taken up as three vertical dividing strips linking to the stuccoed parapet. The right hand bay of the house forms the entrance to French Ordinary Court, a delightfully Dickensian name for a mysterious passageway that tempts the explorer to enter the dingy cavern formed by the arch under Fenchurch Street Station, and which leads to what is sadly our last area.

41, Trinity Square

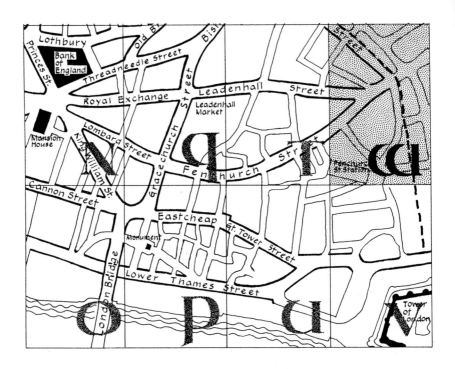

1 Spanish and Portuguese Synagogue
2 St Katherine Cree
3 Sir John Cass School
4 Site of Aldgate
5 Remains of the Holy Trinity Priory
6 Aldgate Pump
7 Lloyds Register of Shipping
8 Site of St Catherine Coleman

a The Three Tuns
b The Cheshire Cheese

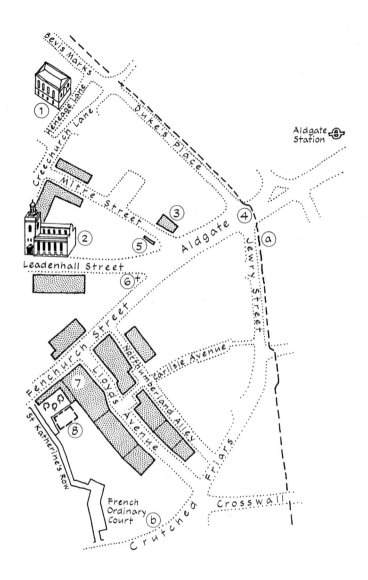

Bevis Marks

Heneage Lane

Duke's Place

Aldgate Station ⊖

1

Creechurch Lane

Mitre Street

3

2

5

Aldgate

4

a

Jewry Street

Leadenhall Street

6 +

Fenchurch Street

Northumberland Alley

Carlisle Avenue

Lloyds Avenue

7

St Katherine's Row

8

Crutched Friars

Crosswall

French Ordinary Court

b

With apologies for leaving you half way down French Ordinary Court, we now carry on to what, as we approach Fenchurch Street, becomes St Katherine's Row. On the right we pass the site of St Katherine Coleman Street, rebuilt in 1739 and sold in 1926, although, as you see, the churchyard still survives. On the corner with Fenchurch Street is the East India public house and, further east, the Lloyds Register of Shipping, a Grade II listed building, designed by T. E. Colcutt and built in 1900. As well as the variety shown in the elevational treatment, we particularly like the frieze depicting rather demure-looking young women holding either model ships or various packages. They were sculpted by George Frampton, and stand under a heavy band between blocked circular columns.

Next we have Lloyds Avenue, created in 1899, with, on the opposite corner, Lloyds Bank of 1900. The buildings in the avenue were originally all of a piece but, since the war, they have unfortunately begun to be eroded. Very nice though is the very elaborate number 4, Coronation House, of 1902. The doorway marks Edward VII's coronation by including a couple of crowns to the balustraded entablature. The crouching lions below seem to be almost an obligatory feature of the period, but are good fun nevertheless. The buildings on this side become progressively more restrained the further down the street we go.

Turning round and looking back up the street, the vista is nicely filled by number 105 Fenchurch Street, in gleaming Portland stone with weathered copper decorations to the mansard. Continuing eastwards along Fenchurch Street we come to the junction with Leadenhall Street and the famous Aldgate Pump, the traditional beginning of the East end. Whilst water had been drawn from this corner since the time of King John, the present pump dates from 1871 and saw only five years of service before the well was closed in 1876. However, all was not lost, because the New River Company then connected their water supply to it. The pump stands alone and forlorn these days, an anachronistic relic of the past, particularly when viewed against the extremely trendy modern bank building that forms its backdrop.

As to Aldgate, the gate that is, it stood at the junction of Duke's Place and Jewry Street on the line of the City wall as can be seen on the map.

Lloyds Register of Shipping

A gate had existed on the site since Roman times, and was rebuilt at the time of King Henry III (1216-72). It was this gate, or rather the accommodation above it, that was leased to Geoffrey Chaucer in 1374. He resided there for twelve years, presumably because it was conveniently situated for his duties as Controller of the Customs of the Port. The gate was the scene of a battle in May 1471 during the Wars of the Roses, when Thomas Neville the 'Bastard of Fauconberg', a cousin of Warwick the Kingmaker (see Area A), attacked the City in the Lancastrian interest with an army of 5,000 Kentishmen. They had passed this way before in 1381 and 1450, having a taste for assaulting London. This time they were not successful and the 'Bastard' retreated. Subsequently the gate was decorated with the heads of two of his captured lieutenants. The gate was rebuilt in 1606 and lasted until 1761 when it was demolished along with the other remaining gates.

Aldgate Pump

On the corner of Leadenhall Street and Mitre Street is Swiss Re House, a large gleaming modern building, and it is with some surprise that one notices through the plate glass of its frontage, a large section of medieval masonry of considerable height. These are the remains of the Holy Trinity Priory, founded in 1104 by Matilda, daughter of Henry I, and dissolved in 1532. Unfortunately, the remains are not open for closer inspection by the public.

Close by we have the Sir John Cass School, the elevation to Mitre Street being particularly charming, a neo-baroque combination of red brick and stone, built in 1910 and designed by A.W. Cooksey, who also designed the altogether larger Institute in Jewry Street, opened in 1902. Sir John Cass, who was born in 1666, was a member of Parliament for the City and was knighted in 1712. He was also Alderman for the Portsoken Ward, in which the schools lie, and left £1,000 at his death in 1718 for the establishment of a school in the ward.

The school in Mitre Street was built on part of the site once occupied by the church of St James Duke's Row, built in 1622-23, which had a reputation for performing marriages without prior bans or licence. The church was demolished in 1874 when its benefice was incorporated in St Katherine Cree which, walking westwards along Leadenhall Street, is our next stop.

St Katherine Cree was built between 1628 and 1632, virtually the same time as St James's, and is a survivor of the Great Fire. The tower is earlier, dating from 1504, and looks as though it should belong to something other than the body with its strictly-proportioned rectangular and rather uncompromising windows. In fact, one could almost say that the western nave window is trying to nudge it out altogether! The church must have looked very modern and novel when first built in the midst of its medieval neighbours.

Creechurch Lane is one of a very few streets in the City that still contain Victorian warehouse buildings. Cree Church Buildings, of 1870s vintage, is attractive with yellow stock bricks and stone window surrounds its hoisting derricks to the upper levels still intact. Numbers 18-20, Cree House, in red brick and stone, is dated 1897. On the opposite corner are some late nineteenth century buildings surrounding Sugar Bakers Court, and that unfortunately is about it. Most of the buildings in the area survived the last war, but not alas its aftermath.

Last, but by no means least in this area is the Spanish and Portuguese Synagogue, designed by Joseph Avis, and built between 1700 and 1701, to replace an earlier one built in Creechurch Lane in 1657. Some of the fittings from this building were transferred to the new one, and Queen Anne donated one of the main roof beams. The entrance is approached via a small courtyard to the north, off Bevis Marks, whilst the southern elevation can be seen in Heneage Lane. The building, in red brick with stone dressings, is simple and well proportioned and remarkably well preserved.

And so with the Synagogue and Bevis Marks we reach the end of our walk around the old City. We do not pretend to have mentioned every old building of note, let alone illustrated them. Fortunately enough still survive to necessitate a book twice this size, and the industry of a new Nicholas Pevsner to list them all. We do hope however that it has acted as an introduction to the subject, and that it will awaken interest in the history of the City and its architecture.

We finish the book with regret, having learned so much ourselves in the process of the research and the writing of it: we will miss it like an old friend. We hope that you too have enjoyed the journey, and that you have shared some of our pleasure in exploring a great city.

POSTSCRIPT

The recent and continuing recession in the building industry has at least brought a halt to the frenzy of demolition and redevelopment that gripped the City in the late 1980s. This was a period when the air was filled with dust, the pavements became obstacle courses for the pedestrian, and the skies were darkened by an ever growing forest of tower cranes that mocked Wren's vision of a City of Spires.

This activity, which at one time threatened to destroy many of the buildings that we have described, was largely brought about by the City's desperate attempt to fight off the challenge for the Capital's financial crown from the rapidly developing Canary Wharf project. In the event neither side won: Canary Wharf stands half empty and the City is now left with a plethora of new office buildings, many unlet. However, in spite of this, still more proposals for office development are in the pipeline waiting for the recession to end.

The positive side of this is that a temporary reprieve has been granted to that which has remained of the older City. It is to be hoped that this breathing space will allow time for proper consideration to be given to long-term developments which recognise the importance of maintaining the architectural heritage exemplified by its listed buildings and conservation areas.

In this book we have on occasion decried the architecture of the post-war period, usually in our opinion justifiably. However, good modern buildings do exist, and if we have not mentioned them it is only because they should properly be the subject of another, different book. Ancient and modern can exist side by side, and there are signs of hope: the refurbishment rather than demolition of Plantation House; the redevelopment of the Lovat Lane and Carter Lane areas and sympathetic new buildings in Cornhill and Austin Friars show that there can be another, better, way of maintaining the character and scale of areas as yet unaffected by large-scale redevelopments.

The City must live and continue to change, it must never become a a museum or, God forbid, a heritage centre. It must however not forget its glorious past and must learn how to achieve that proper balance between the old and the new which is vital if a city is to preserve its soul.

The CITY Churches

All Hallows Barking		U
All Hallows Bread Street	site of	H
All Hallows by the Wall		R
All Hallows Honey Lane	site of	H
All Hallows Lombard Street	site of	Q
All Hallows Staining	tower only	T
All Hallows the Great	site of	O
All Hallows the Less	site of	O
Blanch Apleton Church	site of	T
Christ Church Newgate Street	remains of	F
Collegiate Church of St Martin	site of	H
Dutch Church		R
French Protestant Church	site of	Q
St Alban Wood Street	tower only	G
St Alphage	remains of	L
St Andrew Undershaft		T
St Andrew by the Wardrobe		B
St Ann Blackfriars (churchyard)		B
St Anne and St Agnes		G
St Antholin	site of	K
St Augustine Watling Street	tower only	H
St Bartholomew by the Exchange	site of	N
St Benet Fink	site of	Q
St Benet Gracechurch Street	site of	Q
St Benet Paul's Wharf		D
St Benet Sherehog	site of	K
St Botolph Billingsgate	site of	P
St Catherine Coleman	site of	W
St Christopher-le-Stocks	site of	N
St Clements		O
St Dionis Backchurch	site of	Q
St Dunstan in the East	remains of	U
St Edmund the King		Q

146

St Ethelburga the Virgin	remains	S
St Gabriel Fenchurch	site of	T
St George	site of	P
St Gregory	site of	E
St Helen Bishopsgate		T
St James Garlickhythe		J
St John Baptist	site of	J
St John the Evangelist	site of	H
St John Zachery	site of	G
St Katherine Cree		W
St Laurence Pountney	site of	O
St Lawrence Jewry		L
St Leonard	site of	H
St Leonard Eastcheap	site of	P
St Magnus the Martyr		P
St Margaret Lothbury		N
St Margaret Moses	site of	H
St Margaret on Fish Street Hill	site of	P
St Margaret Pattens		P
St Martin in Ironmonger	site of	K
St Martin Ludgate		B
St Martin Orgar	tower only	O
St Martin Outwich	site of	Q
St Martin Vintry	site of	J
St Mary Abchurch		N
St Mary Aldermanbury	site of	L
St Mary Aldermary		K
St Mary at Hill		P
St Mary Axe	site of	S
St Mary Bothaw	site of	J
St Mary Colechurch	site of	K
St Mary le Bow		H
St Mary Magdalen Milk Street	site of	H
St Mary Magdalen	site of	E
St Mary Mounthaw	site of	I

St Mary Somerset	tower only	I
St Mary Staining	site of	G
St Mary Woolchurch	site of	N
St Mary Woolnoth		N
St Matthew Friday Street	site of	H
St Michael Bassishaw	site of	L
St Michael Cornhill		Q
St Michael Crooked Lane	site of	O
St Michael-le-Querne	site of	E
St Michael Paternoster Royal		J
St Michael Queenhithe	site of	I
St Michael Wood Street	site of	G
St Mildred Bread Street	site of	H
St Mildred Poultry	site of	N
St Nicholas	site of	N
St Nicholas Cole Abbey		H
St Nicholas Olave	site of	H
St Olave Hart Street		U
St Olave Jewry	tower only	K
St Olave Silver Street	site of	G
St Pancras	site of	K
St Paul's Cathedral		E
St Peter by Paul's Wharf	site of	D
St Peter Cornhill		Q
St Peter-le-Poor	site of	R
St Peter Westcheap	site of	H
St Stephen Coleman Street	site of	L
St Stephen Walbrook		N
St Swithin London Stone	site of	O
St Thomas the Apostle	site of	K
St Vedast		H
Spanish and Portuguese Synagogue		W
Trinity Church	site of	H

The Great Fire

THE BLITZ

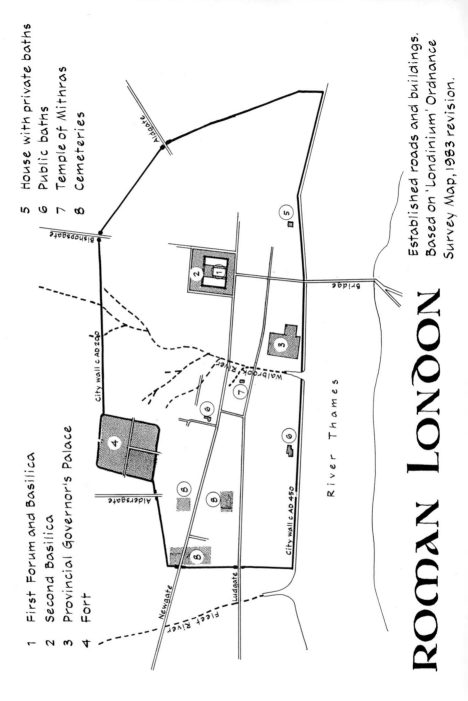

ROMAN LONDON

1 First Forum and Basilica
2 Second Basilica
3 Provincial Governor's Palace
4 Fort
5 House with private baths
6 Public baths
7 Temple of Mithras
8 Cemeteries

Established roads and buildings.
Based on 'Londinium' Ordnance
Survey Map, 1983 revision.

151